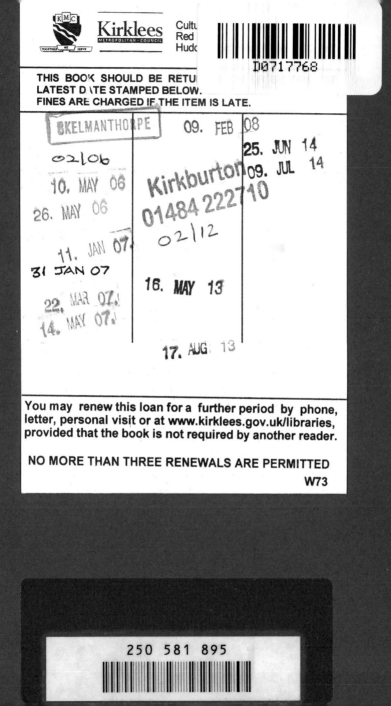

A Lifetime
of
Mountains

THE BEST OF
A. Harry Griffin's Country Diary

Lt Col A. Harry Griffin, Burma Star, ex-14th Army general staff, and Guardian *correspondent for more than fifty years*
(courtesy of Sandra Parr)

A Lifetime
of
Mountains

THE BEST OF
A. Harry Griffin's Country Diary

Edited by
Martin Wainwright

With a foreword by
Chris Bonington

Illustrations by
Clifford Harper

The **Guardian**

A urum

First published 2005 by
Aurum Press Ltd, 25 Bedford Avenue, London WC1B 3AT
www.aurumpress.co.uk
in association with Guardian Books.
Guardian Books is an imprint of Guardian Newspapers Ltd.

ISBN 1 84513 112 6

10 9 8 7 6 5
2009 2008 2007 2006 2005

*The bent but dogged old man of the mountains on p. i was used as a letterhead
by Harry Griffin when he reached his 90s.*

Designed and typeset in Perpetua by Peter Ward

Printed and bound in Great Britain by
MPG Books, Bodmin, Cornwall

'We wished him a lifetime of mountains.'

Country Diary, April 1998

Contents

FOREWORD

H ARRY GRIFFIN was the grand old man of writers about the Lake District. Who can match 60 years of journalism, 53 of them devoted to producing these Country Diaries for the *Guardian* every fortnight without fail? He never wrote with the tone of an old man, however. To the last (and the last was published three days after he died), his brief letters from the hills were fresh and full of zest. He wasn't grand in the conventional sense either, far from it. It was his vision and experience which had the grandeur.

Few people can have spent as much time as Harry Griffin did out on the fells. Of those, hardly any had the skill at rock-climbing that took him into dangerous and lonely places his readers loved to share. He was also exceptionally involved with the people of Lakeland, whether as the local news editor of the *Lancashire Evening Post* or through his many civic, voluntary and sporting activities. It all gave depth and good sense to his writing – and the chance that any of us, his fellow Lakelanders, might suddenly turn up in print on our own breakfast tables. I well remember my own turn: the brief encounter at the back of Skiddaw which he describes overleaf.

These are 150 of the best of Harry Griffin's Country Diaries, but there is a case for saying that any of his contributions to the *Guardian* should be ranked among the best. The 'Best of Harry Griffin' really deserves a series, which would have a great advantage for all of us who hold the Lake District dear. Given that he wrote more than 1500 of these perceptive pieces, we could look forward to a book a year for at least the next decade.

Chris Bonington
July 2005

Brief Encounter
❧ OCTOBER 1980 ☙

To those seeking solitude or somewhere to think, the lonely fells at the 'back' of Skiddaw are always one solution. Here are vast, trackless uplands with views from their summits of the Scottish hills beyond the Solway: miles of emptiness and fresh air where nothing moves except the clouds and the quietly grazing sheep. On a recent round of the 'two thousanders' in this quiet backwater, so different from the rest of the fell country, I saw only one person all day: Chris Bonington, the mountaineer. We met, quite by chance, on the summit of High Pike – he doing a ten-mile jog with his dog 'to sweat out all the beer and all the tensions'. He, too, loves the quietude and the spaciousness of these gentle, sprawling fells; the perfect antidote, perhaps, to the wearing excitements and perils of verticality in distant places. I think it was the first occasion I had met anybody on these lonely tops but, at one time, this countryside must have been alive with activity: the long-abandoned mines; the scattered evidence of early civilizations; and, right on the summit of Carrock Fell, the remarkable ruins of an ancient hill-fort that is still unexplained. For 47 years, a Lakeland shepherd, Pearson Dalton, lived alone with his dogs, goats, and cat at Skiddaw House – perhaps the loneliest habitation in England – but 11 years ago he went into retirement at the age of 75, and the place is now a bothy. Only the sheep now remain in this lonely wasteland where the very absence of tracks, cairns and litter has become the attraction for the connoisseur. Here is the perfect place in which to get away from it all or, in bad weather or low cloud, to practise your compass work.

INTRODUCTION

I FIRST DISCOVERED Harry Griffin when I was a student and he became something of a cult figure among friends who also skim-read the *Guardian*, and enjoyed gently mocking its notorious misprints and the sandal-and-pullover image which its supposed readers had in the 1960s. Distracted by student revolution and all the other heady demands of youth, we parodied Harry's frequent references to solitary days on the fells, the blessed absence of others and the joy of an entire day spent without meeting anyone, except perhaps for Chris Bonington.

Such references certainly recur in Harry's Country Diaries, but they give a misleading impression of the man, who my namesake but not relation, Alfred Wainwright of the guidebooks, sometimes tried to avoid on the tops because he considered him such a chatterbox. When I actually met Harry, in the course of my duties as a fellow *Guardian* journalist, I fell for him immediately. I was 40 and he was 80 but he was a match for anyone in vim, enthusiasm and fun. There was another reason for enjoying his company. He

Harry the reporter, at Lake District sheepdog trials
(courtesy of Sandra Parr)

was unexpectedly not really a *Guardian* man; he took the *Telegraph* for years then switched to *The Times*, buying the *Guardian* only on alternate Mondays so that he could snip out his work (though he did concede that he enjoyed his fortnightly copy and that there was 'something special about the paper'.) With the eagle's nose of a Roman emperor, thick eyebrows and fierce, darting looks from underneath them, he was unquestionably Lt Col A. Harry Griffin, Burma Star, ex-14th Army general staff. He gave vent to vigorous views all round the political and social clock. Although there is nothing finer than a traditional *Guardian* reader, he was different and that made him a breath of fresh air.

Fresh air was what Harry gave to hundreds of thousands of readers for the remarkable 53 years of his stint, through the window which his diaries opened on the magical landscape which he knew backwards and dearly loved. It was warm air too. He was a man who needed company and celebrated community.

He delighted in the beauty of the Lake District and described it perhaps as well as anybody, which is high praise; to walk with giants like Wordsworth and Coleridge. But he knew that it was a place where people lived and had to earn a living. He might accurately describe and deprecate the march of electricity pylons through unspoilt valleys, but he did not expect the dalesfolk to have to live by oil lamplight for ever.

He was also well aware of the paradox that his musings on the uncrowded beauty of the tops did as much as any guidebook to bring in more visitors. Discussing this, he came down firmly on the side of showing the wonder of the Lake District to as many people as possible. He served on the access committee of the old Lakes Planning Board, and would have understood and supported current efforts to attract more ethnic minority visitors, inner-city children and others who do not feature in the statistics as often as they should.

Having emphasized Harry's warmth, I have to mention the time when the *Guardian* photographer Denis Thorpe and I set him on fire. We had taken him up Kirkstone Pass in the snow for a piece to mark his fortieth anniversary as a Country Diarist in 1991, and we were freezing and soaked when we got back to the Queen's Head in Troutbeck for a reviving pint and pie. We got as close to the blazing log fire as we could; too near in the case of Harry, whose anorak suddenly ignited. Luckily Denis and I were not too numbed to put him out.

Fourteen years later, I often think back to that, especially after reading all his Country Diaries, more than 1300 of them, in one concentrated stretch. This is not an experience Harry ever intended but as probably the only person to have done it, I can vouch that the writing stands the test. His themes emerge all the more strongly. The valley he loved best was Dunnerdale (about which, he repeatedly reminds us, Wordsworth wrote 34 sonnets). His favourite fells included humble Whitbarrow and he had a thing about the minute,

March 23   with hes. on skins from Keppel Cove to Whiteside Raise & down.

March 27   Swirral Edge from Greenside. blizzards. abandoned it 100 from the lip owing to ice under powdery snow.

March 29.   Gt. Dun Fell with hes.

March 30   Motoring & walk by Blea Tarn with Nollie.

March 31   Gt Dun Fell — low. Good conditions.

April 4   Gt Dun Fell — very good conditions (alone)

April 5   Gully on Borrowdale Crags (snow climbing) with Ivan Waller. Good day.

April 13–20   Cairngorms.

May 11   Great Gable from Honister ("Leave" — May 16)

May 16   Great End (Cust's) from Grains Gill & Seathwaite Fell (leaves May 23)

May 18   Gt Carrs from Greenburn & climb of Central Buttress

Harry's mountain log: terse jottings which formed
the framework for his crafted diaries
(courtesy of Sandra Parr)

hidden smuggler's cave above Bowfell Buttress, so small that you have to back into it bottom first. He was clear-eyed about the Lake District's problems, but even when grumping about beer-can ring-pulls on the summits or traffic cones in the River Kent, he was optimistic about the landscape's future. He was original too; among the conventional mountain photographs he kept in his desk was a snatch snap by a friend of a flying saucer, or what looks very like one, hovering above Little Arrow Moor.

Harry had an instinct for that sort of oddity, a writer's eye but more specifically a journalist's, full of curiosity and the skill of spotting telling detail. At the foot of his obituary, published in the same paper as his last diary on 12 July 2004, the *Guardian* called him simply 'Journalist'. He would have been pleased about that. One of the stories he liked to tell was how he appeared in court at St Helen's in Lancashire as a young man, after knocking a night watchman into a hole in the road on a late-night drive from Snowdonia. He was banned for six months and the local newspaper reported the case, calling him 'A. Harry Griffin, described as a journalist'. Recalling this, he would pause, chortle and then say: 'Described as! Some doubt, clearly. What do you make of that?'

I would like to thank Harry's daughter Sandra Parr for being so generous with her time and Harry's papers, patiently answering my questions while she carried out the taxing task of clearing her father's flat. Siân Wynn-Jones at the *Guardian*'s Newsroom archive has been an enthusiastic collaborator and Lisa Darnell of *Guardian* Books and Graham Coster and his colleagues at Aurum have given constant cheerful support. The 150 diaries here are mostly in chronological order, adjusted to fit sections with short preludes which I hope add interesting context about Harry's life. And now here he is, doing what he enjoyed most: getting his walking boots on...

Breaking in the boots
NOVEMBER 1979

Good weather recently for breaking in new boots – streaming fells, deep, squelchy bogs and flooded becks. If boots are still painful after a day or two in these conditions they'll never be right. My initial breaking-in was on Wetherlam with pouring rain and thick cloud to complete the cure. Nothing and nobody to be seen, but at least it was comfortable to have dry feet. My old, discarded boots had been letting in water on even moderately damp ground. Before the baptism of the new pair I had soaked them, inside and out, with vegetable oil. In the old days we always used goose grease – carefully saved after Christmas Day by wives or mothers. Dubbin, or mineral oil, we were told, rotted the stitches. Once I broke in a new pair of very stiff, steel-shanked climbing boots by an extremely painful round of the Fairfield Horseshoe. About a mile from the end of the walk I stood knee-deep in Rydal Beck for several minutes until the boots were filled with water, and then fastened the laces as tightly as possible. It was a completely crippling last mile but the boots never gave me the slightest trouble afterwards – once my feet had recovered. The recent floods in the fell country finally put the seal on a disappointing summer and autumn; even the cows, still scratching on the last of the grass, look miserable, although the Herdwicks, long accustomed to hard lying, seem more stoically resigned to their fate. Lawns have never been so matted with moss and everywhere hedges remain uncut. Workers say it has always rained on their precious weekends and several recent glorious Mondays, sandwiched between bad days, can only have added to their desolation.

CHAPTER ONE

Summoned by the *MG*

THE INVITATION ARRIVED in the Lake District on an autumn day in 1950 in an envelope franked at one of the most famous newspaper offices in the world. The editor of the *Manchester Guardian* wondered if A. Harry Griffin would be interested in writing a fortnightly Country Diary to fill the place left by George W. Muller of Cockermouth, a German immigrant, noted rock climber and fox-hunting specialist whose eventful life had recently ended at the age of 75.

The request was an honour for a journalist in provincial England at the time and in Harry's case almost a pinching matter to make sure that it was real. He was a respected journeyman as Northern Editor of the *Lancashire Evening Post* but his reputation didn't go much beyond that. Perhaps he had some name as an inventive broadcaster for the BBC; one of his trainees in Kendal remembers how he covered a flood disaster live from the newspaper's office by opening the window and recording the traffic which sounded the same as the local River Kent in spate. But as Harry enjoyed saying in later years, he couldn't seriously imagine that the *MG*'s then-editor, A.P. Wadsworth, would have noticed that sort of thing; or his weekly 1500-word Leaves From A Lakeland Notebook in the *Post* which, anyway, was only bylined 'Dalesman'.

The *MG*'s Country Diaries were modest, seldom more than 300 words long, but they were given an important place in the paper. Since 1906, when the first of them took over from previously random rural contributions, they had been printed directly below the leading articles – the voice of Manchester Liberalism which on occasion changed governments' minds. Given the size of newspapers at the time, when paper was still rationed, the Country Diary also had a lot of space in relative terms. Harry's first 234 words, on Monday, 8 January 1951, were carried in a paper of only eight pages. Pro rata, in the 88-page paper which published his final contribution on 12 July 2004, he would have had to fill the best part of a broadsheet page.

The Country Diary was also very well read. Back in 1906, the *MG*'s proprietor John Edward Taylor II had asked his editor C.P. Scott if there could possibly be enough material to feed the column, every day all year. He need not have worried. Contributions poured in from the first entry, which recorded the departure of overwintering mallards from a Cheshire mere. So did approval from readers. Very soon, if there was a choice between cutting the less important leaders or the Country Diary to fit the page, it was the leaders that were trimmed.

As a result, country matters attracted star writers. Arthur Ransome was the one of the paper's battlefield and embassy experts in his day, writing from the Russian Revolution, Shanghai and Egypt, but his most devoted followers (until he invented the Swallows and Amazons at his cottage near Coniston Water) were readers of his fishing diary, 'Rod and Line'. Writers of the Country Diary

On honeymoon at the summit of Cairn Gorm, 1937
(courtesy of Sandra Parr)

itself included T.A. Coward who wrote the standard work *British Birds and their Eggs*, and A.W. Boyd, whose book *A Country Parish* ranks beside Gilbert White's *Natural History of Selborne*. They were experts in their fields and readers paid attention to what they wrote.

Harry's was not yet a name to rank with any of these in 1951 but he was well chosen, almost certainly on the recommendation of Muller, who knew the younger man and his passion for the Lakes which, as the old diarist lay dying, were designated as a National Park. Muller read Harry's regional journalism on a day-to-day basis and liked his clear and knowledgeable prose. In turn, Harry looked back on Muller as the best-informed man in Westmorland and the finest fly-fisher in the North of England, quite apart from his skill at rock-climbing and with hounds.

There was another thing in Harry's favour. He always referred, even in his final years, to his first editor as 'Mr Wadsworth' and held him in great respect. But Wadsworth had reached his eminence by self-made means similar to Harry's own. A pipe and a neat moustache were not the only things they shared. Exceptionally for the *Guardian* of his day, where Oxbridge degrees were the norm, Wadsworth finished his formal education at 14, when he left Rochdale higher grade elementary school. He progressed thereafter through his own drive, intellect and boundless curiosity, helped crucially by workers' evening classes in Manchester where his tutor was the historian R.H. Tawney, who became a friend.

Griffin stayed at Barrow-in-Furness municipal high school until 16 but never went to university and hauled himself up by his army bootstraps in the Second World War, from volunteer private to lieutenant colonel in intelligence. He never met Wadsworth, who died in harness in 1955 and was almost always busy with politicians and trade union leaders when not engaged in daily editing. But they would have got on.

In more practical ways, Harry's links with his new employers were tenuous. Communication was entirely by post. The fortnightly Diary was bashed out on a manual typewriter on sheets of paper which Harry adjusted in size so that one diary would exactly fit the page. As the length requested by the paper changed, so did the size of Harry's paper, so that he knew when he was halfway there or within a line or two of the end. The final line almost always shaves the bottom of the paper in his original scripts. His typewriter must have had a good grip.

The finished product was posted off to Cross Street, always from Kendal's main post office and always by Harry in person, in time to arrive without fail for sub-editing at the weekend. In the Wadsworth era, the phone was never used. When Wadsworth's successor as editor, Alastair Hetherington, joined the *Guardian* in 1950, shortly before Harry started, there were no phones in either the Cross Street reporters' room or the 'Corridor', the lofty section where leaders and features were processed, including the Country Diary. It was held that they would disturb the calm and contemplative atmosphere which *Guardian* journalists were thought to need to write.

Harry's first diary appeared below leaders on President Truman's State of the Union address to the US Congress, Soviet foreign policy and the national shortage of coal. Below it was a paragraph unimaginable in today's *Guardian* which told readers that Princess Margaret had attended church in Gullsborough village church and then travelled to Sandringham by car. Harry worked meticulously on his debut piece and to good effect; although it describes only a brief ski descent from the fells it carries two bits of the sort of curious and interesting information on which Wadsworth and the *MG* thrived: the fact that sheep tend to walk in straight lines and that they dig little nests in the snow to crop the grass overnight.

Harry's debut
8 JANUARY 1951

Swiftly and silently, but not particularly expertly, we swooped in great curves down the lower slopes and through the arches to the road and slipped out of our ski bindings by the dry-stone wall which circles the farm. It was quite pleasant to stand upright in the snow for a few moments and, before trudging down to the car, to peep over the old wall which has weathered worse falls than this and see how John's lambing ewes are getting on. There were only about a dozen, all black-faced Rough Fells – the mountain sheep of Westmorland – and against the snow they looked rather like dark boulders somehow missed by the storm. Hard as we stared we could see no movement from any of them, which was not to be wondered at, for each one was quietly cropping from a square foot of grass at the bottom of the little hole she had dug for herself in the snow. But all over the field, criss-crossed like railway lines at a busy junction, were the little hoof-prints of their wanderings and, at the end of each perfectly straight line, the tell-tale cave in the snow. If the snow comes down harder this evening, these are the shelters where the sheep will spend the night, and even if they are 'overblown' it will be warm and cosy inside. John's expectant mothers would take no harm.

On the slate
FEBRUARY 1951

For more than 300 years Lake District men with names like Rigg, Bland, Grizedale and Tyson had been winning Westmorland slate from an enormous crater hidden in the fells, but 20 years ago they decided the quarry was worked out. Recently the old workings have sprung into life again, and, if you climb steeply through the larches and the silver birch, guided by the shrill whirr of the diamond cutter, you will find the young adventurers in their pleasant eyrie – sturdy remnants of a dwindling band of rural craftsmen. Rather a piratical, devil-may-care crew, perhaps; one with a great red beard, another with a wooden leg, and a third with one quizzical eye. But with what precision and dexterity they rive the lovely sea green slate, the best, they say, in England! There are only half a dozen places in the Lake District where you will find slate of this colour, but more than one old roof speaks of its resistance to 200 years of rain and frost.

You reach the floor of the quarry through a tunnel 300yds long, laboriously hacked by hand through the solid rock. The walls of the quarry tower vertically for 300ft, and high above your head you can see where the first tunnel of the seventeenth century pioneers came through.

Badgers versus hounds
⤙ MARCH 1951 ⤚

A lone fell hound, two hours behind the hunt and so weary that he could hardly lift one leg in front of another, crawled down from the steep fellside after a hard day on the 'tops' and steered unerringly for the farmhouse where he had been fed the previous night. As he sank down on the straw in the barn, I saw that he had a nasty badger mark on his jaw.

The badger, no friend of the Lakeland fox-hunter, appears to be on the increase among the woods which skirt the high fells, and several have been killed this winter, but before meeting their end they have often badly punished both hounds and terriers. The other day two game terriers had a terrible battle with a most determined old badger, and then limped uncomplainingly down to the valley with pieces torn out of noses and feet. Without a whimper they submitted to treatment by the red-coated huntsman with disinfectant and salve which must have made the nasty open wounds sting painfully. They will be out of action for some time.

It is mostly after dusk on summer nights when the badger comes out of his hiding in the woods, but he is much too careful to be more than rarely seen. Not long ago I remember one creeping out on to the Windermere-Newby Bridge road and being suddenly illuminated, drinking in a pool, by the headlights of the car.

Merrie Lakeland
❧ JULY 1951 ☙

Fortunately for everybody concerned, the folk-dancing was over before the rains came and we all went home well pleased, our senses tingling with the colour, the rhythm and the music. It would be difficult to find a gathering breathing more of the spirit of 'Merrie England' than a Westmorland folk-dance festival. Picture a long Lake District lawn, sloping gently towards the lake, and on it perhaps 100 garlanded dancers tripping gracefully in the evening sunlight. In the shade of the trees a handful of fiddlers scrape out the old familiar tunes, while the spectators loll near the refreshment tent and ponder on the energy of the performers.

Our festival the other day followed the same pattern except that instead of the lake we had the river, and the fiddlers had been brought out of obscurity and placed in the old bandstand in full view of all. High above the arena the ancient castle ruins looked down on a pattern of colour and symmetry which no doubt appeared much the same 500 years ago.

How dignified and graceful are the old people. That old man with the silver hair must be nearly 80 but his step is still light and his manners still courtly. Perhaps the young men in their garlands, sashes and bells look rather self-conscious, finding the leap back into the Middle Ages a little difficult, but what a delightful picture the carefree children make.

Bilberry feast

AUGUST 1951

High summer has come to Lakeland. The clipped sheep, looking rather shy and naked without their fleeces, stand out almost white against the fellside. The air is full of the splashings, cries and murmurs of becks, birds and insects; the bracken is thickly draped across the hills like a new carpet and the luscious bilberry harvest is there for the picking. How fortunate for the tired and thirsty rock climber that the succulent blue-black berries of this mountain fruit grow mostly on the crags, well out of reach of the commercial picker for, often, after he has belayed the rope on his perch, he can settle down comfortably for a quarter of an hour eating all the bilberries within reach. And bilberries always seem to taste sweetest when you are sprawled in a bed of them, slung far above the valley and just under the clouds. In some places folk call them blueberries or bleaberries and I have also heard them called whortleberries, lingberries or crakeberries. The cranberry, the crowberry, the cloudberry and the bearberry are different sorts of mountain fruits altogether and most of them have no resemblance to the tiny bilberry, looking like a blob of ink among the bright green shoots. Cranberries and crowberries are sometimes picked and sold in Lakeland and the bright red fruit of the cloudberry used to grow near the summit of Bowfell.

Shap shape

These are days of exciting colour in the Lake District – gleaming white snows, skies of Mediterranean blue, the surprising reds, browns and greys of the rocks in new relief, the magical, golden sunset; but there have also been wild nights of almost Arctic severity on the high passes. On the main highway into Scotland, 1400 feet up on the bleak Shap Fells, the snow is lying in drifts several feet deep, and the road itself, darkly zig-zagging through a silent, white world, has at times been as slippery as a glacier. The tough, long-distance lorry men who traverse this road several times a week are not particularly worried about these conditions but when they are met on the summit by a blinding blizzard and cannot distinguish the road ahead from the terrible drop over the edge, they have to stop and ride out the storm somehow. Sometimes the drivers have sat huddled in their draughty cabs waiting for the dawn; other men have left their lorries half buried in the drifts and have staggered knee- or waist-deep in the snow down the steep, twisting miles to the bright lights of the Jungle Café, which every driver knows. And all through these long, wild nights roadmen from the valleys have been working bravely, their gloved hands freezing to their spades, to keep the great road, main artery of Westmorland and the North, open at all costs.

The egg men

The cloak-and-dagger men of the fells, the egg-collectors, have been about their bold, bad business recently, so there will be fewer young ravens and peregrines in Lakeland this summer than Nature had planned. Each weekend during the nesting season these men have been roping down overhangs to the wild eyries of these fine mountain birds and pocketing the whole clutch every time. Sometimes they are working for a collector from outside the district, often the eggs are sold for big money, and occasionally the man on the rope is an enthusiast interested only in the eggs, not the cash. No doubt some of them would prefer it to be noised abroad that the peregrine has forsaken the Lake District, but this is fortunately not so. The raven has been nesting in most of his usual 'stations' but we do not hear much of the 'red' raven nowadays. This was the fabulous bird which used to nest in a crag in Oxendale, at the head of Great Langdale, almost in the shadow of Crinkle Crags. She came back to the same wild spot, or near it, as ravens do, year after year, but unlike other ravens, she laid red-coloured eggs. I have seen, in a lamplit room, behind drawn curtains, 16 clutches of these eggs – probably the only collection of its kind in existence. Forty pounds would not buy just one of these clutches. When the glass lid was carefully taken off the tray I was not allowed to touch the eggs and scarcely allowed to breathe.

Revenge on the fox
❧ JUNE 1952 ❧

We were standing on a jagged tumble of huge boulders below the soaring walls of Esk Buttress and one of the three weather-tanned dalesmen – looking, with their guns and grim faces, rather like Corsican bandits – pointed with his weapon. 'Sitha! Yon's wheer t'cubs ev bin playin'. This is't spot aw reet.'

Sure enough, a tiny shelf of grass hidden among the rocks had been newly trampled down, and down a dark hole near the fox cubs' playground lay the pitifully mangled remains of three tiny lambs.

The dalesman wasted no time with words. 'Put terriers in, Ben,' he commanded and, eager for battle, three brown, wiry terriers wriggled down into the unknown darkness of the foxes' lair. In the silence, guns at the ready, the men waited for the foxes to bolt, but nothing emerged except little Jeff who popped up from another hole three yards away, found another likely-looking crevice, and disappeared for another search. And for an hour or more, without a sound, the terriers scurried in and out of the borran far below our feet. Only once, from the distant depths, we heard a savage scuffle and a strangled cry, but whether the little chaps had found the old fox or the cubs or merely one another, we did not know.

We had to leave the men to their grim, essential task, but later, from half a mile away down the valley, we heard two quick shots. Perhaps a dozen lambs had been avenged.

Stormy treasure
July 1953

The other afternoon when the shade temperature had crawled into the eighties, nature went beserk in one quiet corner of our countryside and within two hours did more damage than a thousand men could do in a week. One moment the fells were steaming in the sunshine, sheepdogs drowsing in the shade, and shirt-sleeved roadmen grumbling about the heat as they worked on the pass. Within half an hour, hailstones as big as pigeon's eggs were falling out of the skies, huge trees were being wrenched out by their roots, boulders many tons in weight were crashing down the hillside and great floods were carving out new ravines and tearing up walls and roads as they surged, in boiling, brown fury, down to the valley. Tonight the local council is meeting to see what can be done about the damage. Nobody who saw the storm will ever forget that afternoon, but already the roads are partly repaired, the flooded homes and ravaged fields may recover in time and the country folk will return to normal life again. But the new scars on the fellside will remain for ever. One new ravine awaits examination by experts. Black, shining rock, hidden under soil and bracken for thousands of years, has been exposed by the gouging floodwater and may be a seam of graphite. So far the only graphite found in the Lake District was at Seathwaite in Borrowdale, and they said that this was the purest graphite in the world. One hundred and twenty years ago, when you could buy a sheep for about four shillings, this graphite sold at forty-five shillings a pound, but the old mine has not been worked for generations.

War on the ants

❧ APRIL 1953 ❧

A very rough estimate of the number of ants in my lawn is anything between 10,000 and, say, half a million. There certainly seem to be many more than there were last year, in spite of a systematic slaughter which went on for months. For some reason, ants prefer my lawn to those of any of my neighbours, which are completely ant-free. Perhaps my grass is more succulent or the underlying soil more suitable for burrowing purposes. Every type of powder designed for the extermination of ants has been tried but no matter what their losses, they come back refreshed, in greater numbers, to wreak their daily havoc. Is it possible, I sometimes wonder, that ants can get so accustomed to deadly powders that in time they can actually thrive on them? One powder I tried was of a very special type. It was said that it paralysed the ants so that they lost their senses and, instead of escaping, foolishly entered into the heaviest concentrations and ultimately perished. Rather like the elaborate machines for killing flies, once you have caught them, but I had reached the state in which I was prepared to try anything. But the only effect the joke powder had on my ants was to give them such perspicacity that they could be seen, great droves of them, carrying their eggs to safety and even dragging off their unconscious comrades, presumably to apply artificial respiration in some subterranean hideout. The next thing I tried, in desperation, was boiling water, which killed off the ants alright, but also finished off the grass. This year the grass is coming back, and so are the ants – whole divisions of them and fatter than ever.

Whistling Jack
❧ SEPTEMBER 1953 ☙

Old Jack Thistlethwaite – Whistling Jack to anybody who knows him – has just been presented with a walking stick for being 'the most remarkable farm worker in England'. He is 87 years of age, and has been planting potatoes, cutting hay, spreading manure, laying hedges, digging drains and so on for 77 years. They say that he has never had a day's illness in his life and he is probably the happiest man in Westmorland.

On the day of the presentation Old Jack, who has a brown, crinkled face and looks about 70, got up early as usual – he is a bachelor and used to cooking his own meals – and walked nearly three miles to the farm where he works, getting there just before 8a.m. After about six hours' work in the harvest field he went along to the show ground in his shirt sleeves, soiled trousers and decrepit old hat, and after the presentation, which he had dreaded for days, he trotted out of the arena as quickly as he could. There were plenty of people anxious to talk to him, buy him a drink or show him round the exhibits, but although it was a lovely day for idling in the sunshine and the leaping contests were in full swing Old Jack could not be tempted. 'I want to git back to me work,' he said and off he went.

His boss swears he is the best worker he ever had, and says he has never yet given him an order. The old man just stays on the job until there is no more work to do and then he walks the three miles home for his supper. They say he is too happy to retire.

Meeting owls
⌁ MAY 1954 ⌁

Until quite recently I had never met any owls of any kind socially, but within a week or two I have made acquaintance with two of the tawny variety, becoming almost intimate with one of them. Hitherto, I had only been able to obtain even a sight of owls by creeping quietly up to well-known haunts, making a noise, and watching them fly out, but the other day in a quiet Westmorland lane I saw one sitting jauntily on a garden fence. As he did not fly away as the car passed, I stopped, backed up to the fence and had a good look at him from a distance of about two feet. We sat staring at each other for several minutes and then, getting bored at the sight of my face, the owl flew away, apparently in disgust. My next meeting was in a former shooting lodge in Scotland. We were seated round the fire one evening when we heard a peculiar screeching sound at the window, and there was a tawny owl, blinking at the light. When we had got over our surprise and as the owl showed no signs of leaving, we opened the window and he hopped into the room on to the back of a chair. Half an hour later, after several photographs had been taken, he was still there and we were feeding him with bits of bacon rind. He had apparently been a weakly fledgling and had been cared for by the people of the house, since when he often came back for food. They called him 'Frankie', short for Frankenstein, and in some lights he looked rather frightening. He certainly did about five o'clock the following morning when I was awakened by his screeching and found him perched at the foot of my bed. After a bad ten minutes persuading him to leave I went back to bed – with the windows closed.

Cragfast

MARCH 1955

There's an old Lakeland theory that the best way to deal with a cragfast sheep is to leave her on the crag until she wastes away into a bundle of wool. You then simply push her over the edge, and she will float safely down to earth. We thought rather enviously of this simple, if slightly inhumane, method the other day when we were wrestling with two of them above a 200 foot overhang. The farmers said the sheep had been up there three weeks but, judging by their strength, determination and agility, it seemed likely to be many more weeks before they were fit for the parachute method. They seemed perfectly content, snatching at the odd tuft of grass wedged in a crevice, until you got near enough with the rope. Their only thought then was to leap over the edge – if possible, dragging you with them. You might get a loop round one of their necks and have high hopes – while almost swinging in mid-air – of getting the forelegs in as well, when suddenly she would be out of the noose and slithering over the edge, with her former foothold crashing on to the screes below. These were the moments when one's own lifeline looked woefully thin.

I don't know what we'd have done if they had been of the horn-less variety. As it was, we discovered that a pair of horns makes an excellent belaying pin and that once one was lashed to a convenient root, you could begin to think out the next move. These two fought hard all the way down even when, as often happened, they were hanging upside down. Even when they were safe on the screes, with comfortable grazing close at hand, they glared at us and seemed to look longingly at their remote ledge.

The Campbells are going
◈ MAY 1959 ◈

The speed kings have finished with this lovely lake for ever – or so we are told – and Coniston Water is left with its occasional patch of sail, its handful of rowing boats and its char. It has been a 20-years-long story, this saga of record-breaking on one of the least-spoiled of the English Lakes, but very soon, when the boathouse, the crews, caravans, the advertisements and the great ugly cranes have gone, there will be little to remind us of the adventure. Perhaps the little post at each end of the measured kilometre will be left, but that will be all. Years ago people used to complain about the noise – the peace of Lakeland was being disturbed – but their voices are no longer heard and, indeed, the explosions at the slate quarries are louder. The record seekers have perhaps brought in their wake a touch of ugliness and vulgarity, but that will soon be forgotten, while the rare beauty of a silver-blue flash streaking like an arrow along the mirrored lake in the morning sunlight will long be remembered. Today this straggling almost-Alpine village which 20 years ago welcomed the young man's father is a little sad, and not only because the golden egg has disappeared. A breath of the exciting, outside world had blown into the Fell country – and they liked it.

The violin maker
◈ NOVEMBER 1960 ◈

In the attic of a house in a Lakeland village, a little man is hard at work from dawn till night making violins. Through his tiny roof window he can see a line of crags and above them the sky, but he has no time to look at the scenery for he has so much work to do. He is up at six o'clock, summer and winter, weekdays, and

Sundays, and never puts down his tools before ten o'clock at night. Every year he makes four violins, fashioning each part, except the strings, with his own hands. Even his tools he made himself, and he scorns the use of machinery. You can buy violins made in a factory, the wood bent by steam, but the instruments made by this Lakeland craftsman are not ordinary violins. Each one is an exact copy of the great Italian masters, with the curves carved and not bent, and many famous violinists have told the little man what remarkably fine copies they are. I asked him the obvious question: 'How do you get this wonderful tone?' and I got the obvious reply: 'That's my secret.' But he was prepared to tell me part of the story. Most of the secret, it seems, is in the varnishing – at least a six months' job – and the rest is in the tuning of the back of the violin. And so, for hours at a time, this little man is tapping away at his thin pieces of wood, listening to the sound, taking off a shaving, and listening again. A craftsman, certainly, but I suggest an artist as well. And he seems to have only one relaxation – playing the violin.

CHAPTER TWO

Into His Stride

W<small>HO WAS</small> A. Harry Griffin? He was born Arthur Harold Griffin on 15 January 1911 in Liverpool but moved as an infant to Barrow-in-Furness, where his parents set up a decorating business. They were more likely to climb ladders than mountains, but Harry and his younger brother, Leslie, were taken scampering up Black Combe and other Lakeland outliers from the age of eleven. Their dad, ever liable to get lost, led some expeditions and their school's junior mountaineering club the others. 'Never drink from becks, boys,' was their teacher's motto. 'It will affect your wind.'

They were encouraged to look outward, too, by Barrow's place as a port and shipbuilding centre. Everyone in Harry's childhood seemed to have a connection with the sea. One uncle was an officer in the merchant navy; another worked in the shipyard and took submarines across the Atlantic to Chile. With the sea came romance.

And in the 1920s there was nowhere more romantic than the icebound waters of the Antarctic and the great British heroes they created, especially Sir Ernest Shackleton.

Harry absorbed the explorer's story in Barrow library, particularly the account of Shackleton's dauntless journey in an open boat and across the unmapped, snow-covered mountains of South Georgia to get help, when his ship the *Endurance* was wrecked in Antarctica in 1916. The adventure books were next to the library's section on climbing, and that started a lifelong love affair for Harry. But in a more general sense, his reading determined him to get out into the world.

His father was a friend of the editor of the weekly *Barrow Guardian* and Harry's obvious enthusiasm led to the offer of a cub reporter's job in 1928. After four years' training, he applied for senior status but the paper could not afford the rise in pay. So he took the train to Preston and talked himself into a job on the *Lancashire Evening Post*. From there he was soon translated to Manchester and the Northern office of the *Daily Mail*, where he showed another journalistic quality, guile. As an accomplished pianist, he was keen to hear the Hallé Orchestra as often as possible but, like any good Northerner, without paying through the nose. So he persuaded the *Mail* to make him Northern music critic in addition to his reporting duties. He met scores of famous musicians including Rachmaninov, cockily telling the great man that he had taken the final movement of his Third Symphony too fast. To his lasting regret he never got to know the celebrated Neville Cardus, music critic of the *MG*, because he always had to rush from concerts to meet his *Mail* deadline. But he was the only journalist to interview Sir Thomas Beecham in the nude.

'I was fascinated by his pink, diminutive body, his jaunty beard and the curious Turkish slippers, with curved, pointed toes, which he proceeded to put on – before his dressing gown,' he remembered, after arriving early at Beecham's hotel, opening the wrong door and finding himself in the bathroom as the conductor

Like father, like son: Arthur Griffin on Coniston Old Man
(courtesy of Sandra Parr)

was getting out of the bath. All was set fair for a headline-making career but, like all his generation, Harry and his plans were overwhelmed by the Second World War. Three years after he started on the *Mail* in 1937, he was in the uniform of a volunteer private in the Cheshire Regiment, where he won an officer's commission and transfer to the Royal Artillery and then the Intelligence Corps.

Harry was modest about his military career, claiming that the high point came at a Kentish outpost when he was the nearest British officer to Nazi-occupied Europe. He was moved to Scapa Flow naval base in Orkney where he became an intelligence expert on German fleet dispositions and then, armed with this knowledge, was relocated to Burma. He took part in the successful defence of Imphal which turned the tide against the all-conquering Japanese. He nearly fell out of an aircraft on a supply drop behind enemy lines, suffered minor injuries when he was at an ammunition dump which blew up, and posed in triumph on a knocked-out Japanese tank. When he was demobilised, he was Lieutenant Colonel A. Harry Griffin and he looked it.

This was invaluable when he returned to journalism and the *Mail* in Manchester, which wanted to move him to London with other high-flyers whose career had been put on hold by the war. But Harry didn't like big cities and had decided to get back to the Lake District, to climb, write and bring up his small son and daughter in idyllic surroundings. The question was: who would pay him to do this?

The answer was his old paper the *Lancashire Evening Post*, when Harry bumped into a pal who tipped him off that the paper was looking to expand into the Lakes. Knowing that the new editor was a disliked tyrant, Harry put on his full uniform complete with medals for an interview where, he said later, 'the awful little squit practically stood at attention'. He negotiated a salary so special, by the mean standards of British regional journalism, that he had to sign a written agreement to keep it confidential.

So began a journalist's dream, a working beat of rare beauty and interest, and in time the stimulating responsibilities of working as the *Post*'s Northern editor with younger reporters and trainees to encourage. Harry started a column, Leaves from a Lakeland Notebook, which he was to contribute weekly without a gap for the next 46 years (most of them in tandem with his *Guardian* pieces, which never dealt with the same subject). And he was present at almost all the region's major news events.

These included a terrible mining disaster at the William Pit in Whitehaven in 1947 which killed 140 men, and, most notably, the death of Donald Campbell on Coniston Water in 1967 when his *Bluebird* speedboat somersaulted at around 300mph. Harry scooped the world on this tragedy, through his close personal links with Campbell and his nous about where to station himself during the record attempts. The ex-officer and bold climber clicked naturally with Campbell who took him out during 120 mph trials, the only journalist ever to ride in *Bluebird* and briefly, 'uncomfortably and frighteningly', he was the eighth fastest person on water in the world. On the day of the tragedy, while other journalists went up the lake to the mile-post, Harry stayed at Campbell's base, watching through binoculars and listening to the crackly ship-to-shore radio. When this suddenly went dead and Harry saw a cloud of spray through his binoculars, he realized what had happened. He sprinted to Campbell's private caravan, phoned the BBC in London and broke the news to the world.

This was Harry's parallel life to the scrambles on the fells which he recorded in the *Guardian*, but the two were closely connected. As A.P. Wadsworth had foreseen, a good journalist's eye was invaluable in spotting subjects to write about for the Country Diary, and a good journalist's prose made the paragraphs – from moss hunters to a stubbornly shy pigeon – come alive.

Inspector Moss
MARCH 1958

It is natural that a detective should spend his working hours tracking down criminals, but perhaps a little unusual that he should use his leisure in tracking down – of all things – rare mosses. There is such a man in our lake counties, a large plain-clothes officer with the look of a successful judge of, say, fat cattle. When constabulary duties are done he likes nothing better than to scramble up some steep, dirty gully in a remote part of the fells, seeking tiny plants so small that most of us would never even see them. But once he has collected his specimens, his work takes on something of the aura of that of the detective of fiction, for he gets to work in a book-lined study at home with his microscope. The beauty of even the smallest wild flowers is apparent to most of us, but the beauty in a tiny shred of moss is only revealed under the microscope when the keen bryologist can study the amazingly varied leaf cell formations – perhaps one thousandth of an inch in diameter – and even count the tiny globules of chlorophyll clustered inside them. Here is a new world of beauty, completely hidden from all except a comparatively few enthusiasts. But it is not only beauty which our detective seeks in his precious hours off duty, but also the thrill of discovery. Four times he has discovered mosses never before recorded in Cumberland and once he has done the same for Westmorland. Lake District mosses still 'undiscovered' had better look out.

Calm and storm
JUNE 1960

The storm lasted less than half an hour but in that time completely changed the appearance of the hills. It had been a hot stifling day with a steamy haze hanging over the fells and the tarn so still you could see the minnows ten feet down. Half-way through our third climb we heard the distant thunder and decided to call it a day, but there seemed no need for haste. We hardly noticed the sun go in and the sky darken and we had coiled the rope and trotted half-way down the screes before we met the wind. A dry, rampaging sort of wind it was, blowing the dust up in our faces, chasing round the corrie, and churning the tarn into a whirlpool. The thunder was much nearer now and the lightning flashes much more frequent. Two-thirds of the sky was an angry blue black and the remainder an ominous-looking orange. We quickened our steps but we were only half-way across the moor when a vicious jab of lightning almost blinded us and a great crash of thunder directly overhead seemed to rock the fellside. The first rain spattered on the dusty rocks and then the quick rat-tat-tat of hail and, within seconds, we were in the middle of a deluge. In its way it was invigorating and even entertaining for once you are wet through to the skin – this took about half a minute – there is no real discomfort. Within minutes the dried-up fellside was live with a hundred rivers and we splashed down and along them, knowing we could get no wetter, while the torrent poured down, hailstones and bathtubfuls of them, the lightning flashed and the thunder crashed and rolled. A good end to a good day.

Wrestling boys
August 1960

The farm lad in Cumberland and Westmorland, particularly if he lives within reach of one of the 'academies', doesn't waste too much of his spare time tinkering about with motorbikes or going into the nearest town. He gets down to his wrestling. For there's much more to this business than sheer brute strength. It is indeed a highly technical game and a smallish man who knows what he is about can often topple some great hulking fellow, nearly twice his weight. The secret is to tempt your opponent into a position of apparent security and then, quickly, to get him off balance. To the outsider knowing something of the game the slow circling of the greensward, with the two wrestlers locked together, may seem a waste of time, a playing to the gallery, but it is nothing of the kind. The men are waiting for the slightest sign of relaxed concentration on the part of their opponent, and the moment one attacks, the other must be ready with his move. You don't defend yourself in Cumberland and Westmorland wrestling, you counter-attack; otherwise you are down. It is an ancient sport, a manly sport, and in these days when betting tends to spoil so many outdoor events, a surprisingly clean sport. A young lad can practice at the 'academy' in the wintertime, and stand a chance, the next summer, of becoming the 'champion of the world' at his weight. And dozens of 18-year-olds from the dales have achieved this distinction.

Roman remains

ᐸᑭ SEPTEMBER 1960 ᑫᐳ

Nearly 2000 years have passed since the Romans stood on this same spot and looked down, as I am looking now, along the green, flat valley to the sea and northwards to the highest land in England. Little has changed over the centuries – a little less woodland today on the lower slopes, perhaps, rather more bracken and the stone walls marching over the fells, but still the same shapes peeping through the clouds, the same winding track over the pass, the same tumbled, black crags, the ravines and the tremendous solitude. How many times, I wonder, as I stand inside the fort, shoulders hunched against the driving rain, had the Romans stood up here on just such another evening, watching the storm clouds gather over

Scafell and sadly thinking of their distant, sunny homeland? Four sodden Herdwicks, cropping the grass inside the fort, share my vigil and now and again one of them will shake itself in a cloud of spray. A pair of ravens wheel high above the pass but the winding road is deserted and the only sound comes from the flooded becks. Down to the left, below the muddied track, are the remains of the baths where the soldiers steamed and behind me was their exercise ground. The commandant's office was straight ahead and the four watch towers are plain to see. Today, almost within sight of the world's first atomic power station, they are 'restoring' this link with our earliest days, uncovering the old walls, putting each stone back in place. With so much ahead of us, the past has suddenly become important.

Mountain cat

April 1961

On several occasions I've written about my mountaineering dog, but now — for the first time — I've discovered a mountaineering cat. He's a Siamese called Rikki and seems to be the constant companion on the fells of a local mountaineering schoolmaster. Recently, however, Rikki suffered his first defeat, being beaten after a week's siege of the peak, by deep, slushy snow on the upper slopes of Ben Nevis, the highest mountain in Britain. Not that Rikki hadn't trained hard for his first 'four thousander'. He'd done several tops in the Lake District without oxygen or other artificial aids and thought nothing of them, but the soft snow into which he disappeared at every step on the upper slopes of the Ben proved a different matter. And the final indignity — quietened with a bromide and carried down asleep in a rucksack — will not easily be forgotten. For Rikki is a mountaineer in the proper tradition, well equipped and accustomed to living off the country. He has his own little sleeping bag for high-altitude camping and on the Ben did his own hunting – of mice – among the boulders near the camp site at 2000ft. While acclimatizing himself for the summit bid he would disappear into his own private caves among the boulders and only emerge, tired-out and well-fed, at bedtime. It was, thought Rikki, a wonderful week – why climb mountains when you can hunt all day? – but his master was disappointed. The other day, however, came some consolation, for Rikki ticked off Helvellyn by way of Swirral Edge without batting a whisker.

Stone age
OCTOBER 1961

Just a few feet away from the well-marked track to a popular crag is a rough circle of stones where, nearly 4000 years ago, the people who lived on this lonely moor before the dawn of history held strange rites and buried their dead. Few of the climbers who regularly pass this way know the spot, for it is only when you are standing in the very centre of the ring that you realise the significance of the stones. From the track they look just the same as the thousands of rocks which lie tumbled across every fellside. The other day I stood in the rain in the centre of the circle as I have often done before, try-ing to picture these people of the mist of so long ago and wondering what really happened in this desolate place between the mountains and the lake. The stones make as perfect a circle as you could draw with a stick and a long piece of string, there is nothing accidental about them, and, from the centre, you can detect openings north, south, east and west. Human sacrifices? I don't know. But just over 50 years ago they dug up the place and discovered urns, a piece of charred woollen stuff, a clay bead, some human bones and a tiny cup containing a baby's tooth. Perhaps the antiquarians can guess at the meaning of it all – a Bronze Age cemetery, perhaps, or a sacred spot where the gods were appeased – but on a wet October day with the mists swirling across the fell it seemed important just to realise that it all happened before the days of Helen of Troy.

Pigeon post
MAY 1963

Not all of us are as good with pigeons as Mr Francis Chichester who took one part of the way across the Atlantic. For the past two hours I have been trying to coax one into my house without success. He landed just after lunch at the foot of the steps leading to my front door – two miles out of town and, so far as I know, remote from any loft – and he's still there. When I get near him he hops or flies away – but only for a yard or two. By cunning strategy – a long trail of breadcrumbs – I got him all the way up the steps, 12 of them, to the porch, and have had him drinking out of a saucer, but so far he has evaded capture. Either I'm going about it in the wrong way – I know less about these birds than almost any others – or he doesn't like the look of Sambo, my Border Collie, who is looking at him rather fiercely through the window. Sambo has never seen one of these before, and I must say I've never examined one as closely as this, although dozens of them camp out on the ledges of the town hall two or three miles away. After half a slice of bread and several drinks of water, both from my saucer and from pools on rocks in the garden, the pigeon has retreated to the third step where he sits very patiently, chest swelled up, looking out at the rather fine view.

It's drizzling now but he doesn't seem to be bothered. Every now and again he cocks a very perky eye at me as if to say, 'Hey, you, I'm back.' Obviously he's not injured; probably he's just tired. Perhaps he's flown over from France this morning but can't remember the last few miles home. Now, who's the local expert on racing pigeons?

Drystone walls

JUNE 1963

I've seen a couple of farm lads put up seven yards of respectable drystone walling in a day, but a similar length of walling at my house has taken two craftsmen the best part of three weeks. Indeed, it went up so slowly, this terrace wall, that from day to day you could hardly detect any advancement in the work. One might almost have been watching one of the labours of Hercules, but in fact this bit of wall is only three feet high at one end, gradually reducing to three inches at the other.

Of course, there are different sorts of Lake District walling. With an ordinary field wall you just take the stones that are to hand and fit them together with no more than an occasional chipping with the hammer, but this wall of mine had to be built in dressed limestone and each piece carved out with old-fashioned skill. The biggest job was not in building the wall but preparing the stone, and for days there was great play with rulers, plumb-bobs, spirit-levels and pieces of string. And the stone had to be the right sort of colour; mine came from a newly-demolished ancient building at £3 a ton plus cartage.

In the end my wall is not a drystone wall at all, although it looks like one. Like other Lake District walls it is really two walls cleverly joined together by 'throughs,' but unlike the ordinary field wall it has mortar tucked away out of sight, so that it not only looks solid but should also outlast my lifetime. We fixed a coping on top, so that the vexed question of cam-stones – whether they should be castellated or diagonal or smoothed over with cement – did not arise. It's been a long and doubtless expensive job, but a once shabby corner has been transformed and I can now sit in comfort on my terrace and watch the sun going down behind the Langdale Pikes.

Fell pony
❧ NOVEMBER 1963 ☙

A young Fell pony from the Westmorland hills has gone to the Royal stud at Balmoral – at the request, it is stated, of the Queen. It was George V who first introduced Fell ponies to Balmoral and now they fit easily into the Highland scene. It may not be generally realised that Cumberland and Westmorland has its own native breed of pony, as indigenous to the district as the red deer and as distinctive a breed as the Shetland.

Fell ponies are much bigger than Shetlands and at 13 to 14 hands high are perhaps only exceeded in size by the Highland pony. You can still find a few of them running wild in the fells and living the life their ancestors led 2000 years ago, but most of them are now registered and in private ownership, mainly in the north, but some of them scattered to all parts and even overseas. You might spot them on High Street or north of Helvellyn – rugged-looking individualists, either black or brown, with long, shaggy manes and tails. When met high up in the fells in wild weather, they appear dark, unkempt, and rather fierce. But in fact they are the most docile of creatures and when groomed can appear quite sleek. They say that the first Fell pony to be given a proper name was found, with trailing rein, cropping the heather on the slopes of Stainmore after the remnants of the '45 had straggled through Westmorland. Whether he had been ridden by Scot or Englishman nobody knew, but they took him down to one of the farms and, for want of a better name, called him 'Ling Cropper'. And the same name persists throughout the breed to this day.

Woodsmoke
↢ FEBRUARY 1965 ↣

One of the fanciful attractions of the townsman for the country is the smell of woodsmoke. The memory of a few fragrant whiffs inhaled when he drops down to the farm in the valley after a winter's day in the fells is enough to make the man, looking out over crowded rooftops, sigh for lost days in the open air among friendly dalesfolk. The scent of woodsmoke for him can be as nostalgic as the sight of his tattered rucksack and boots, an old map or faded photographs of carefree hours. I live in the country, two miles from a market town, but I burn logs on my drawing room fire basically for economy reasons. In theory it sounds all right. Whenever you see a dead branch you put it in the back of the car and then cut it up on your electric saw. But in practice it never works out that way. You either have to grow trees and cut them down or you have to buy them or loads of logs.

I once bought a tree or rather its branches – the owner had the trunk – for £5 and it lasted me all winter, but the logs were far too big to go on the fire and had to be split with immense labour. Nowadays I get a load from the a farmer at about the same cost but there's still a lot of axing to be done, as well as carting and stacking, and each night the fire consumes a wheelbarrow load of logs. My latest pile is the chopped remains of a big dead ash that I persuaded the farmer needed felling, but the heap is dwindling rapidly. It smells wonderful from the garden – if you care to venture out on a winter's night – but you don't notice it much inside. But now I'm growing my own firewood, although it may be ten years at least before the trees are ready for thinning.

Madcap pilots
ꙮ FEBRUARY 1966 ꙮ

The Helvellyn memorials have been in the news recently and the other day one of them, the so-called 'Hinkler' memorial, was dragged down the mountainside on a sledge so that it can be refurbished, or fettled up, as we say in these parts. This simple stone plaque commemorates the occasion 40 years ago when an aeroplane was landed on the summit, but while they are about it they might like to get the name right. For Hinkler, the Australian pilot who was later, ironically enough, to be killed when his plane flew into a mountainside, neither landed the plane on Helvellyn nor took it off again. The pilot and originator of the madcap scheme, in fact, was a North of England pioneer of aviation, John F. Leeming, who also wrote books on gardening and bees, and Hinkler was his passenger. It was simply a stunt to popularize civil aviation and it was finally achieved, after several abortive attempts, on 22 December 1926, a cold wintry day with snow on the hills.

One of the most extraordinary features of a remarkable flight was that, in spite of the weather, there was – quite by accident – a witness of the landing, a professor of Greek at Birmingham University who knew nothing about the flight but had merely gone up the mountain alone for some winter exercise. What were his thoughts as he was contemplating the view from the cairn when the Avro two-seater dropped down out of the skies and landed beside him one can only guess. Anyway, he was able to sign a certificate scribbled out on an old bill he found in his pocket that a landing had been made, and a few moments later the airmen were off again. They only had about 30 yards in which to get airborne and beyond that the screes and precipes dropping down to Red Tarn, but they just did it and history, of a sort, had been made.

Summer nights
ᐛ JULY 1966 ᐝ

With a full moon this weekend and as I write the hills smiling in the evening sunlight, we are right in the middle of the 'watching-the-sunrise' season. To see the wonder of the dawn at its best there is no finer viewpoint that the top of a high hill, and Helvellyn is so suitable and accessible that it has become known as the 'sunrise mountain'. So that most weekends about this time of the year, when the skies are clear and there is promise of a sunny day, you will find people of all ages perched near the cairn waiting in the darkness for the dawn. They walk up in the night hours from Wythburn or Thirlspot or, if there is sufficient moon, over the rock towers of Striding Edge, and then settle down around the ruined shelter out of the wind with their flasks of coffee and maybe a chicken sandwich or two.

Often they are disappointed, for a clouded sky will ruin the effect, but if they are lucky they will see a pageant of the skies they will long remember. For some time before the dawn, the eastern sky glows a rich orange and gradually grows lighter until around five o'clock the sun suddenly peeps over the Pennines and all at once it is a new day. In a few moments the cold lunar light with the hills in black silhouette and the moon shining on distant waters changes to the warm glow of a perfect sunny morning, and the golden rim of the sun swells into a huge ball of fire bathing the whole of the Lake District in new friendly colour. Far to the north-west you can see the Lowland hills of Scotland and there are long black shadows across the turf. The night is forgotten and you run down the fellside for breakfast feeling that somehow you have stolen an extra day.

Bones of the past
৫৬ JUNE 1968 ৩৯

The most striking change that has come over the Lake District in the past few hundred years – apart from the invasion of the motor car – is, remarkably enough, its decline as an industrial area. Many of us forget that the district was once thickly spattered with mines, quarries, iron furnaces, woollen mills, gunpowder works and the like, but an exhibition of old drawings, engravings and photographs at Ambleside this week tells much of the story. The fells and the lakes, the woods and the waterfalls are still the same but the foregrounds to the pictures have changed. Modern photographs placed alongside the old pictures show the open fields, lake shores and lower fellsides that the tourist knows so well, but the mills, water wheels and bits of assorted machinery captured by the old artists have long disappeared. There was a time when the woods were people with charcoal burners and swill makers and an army of a thousand men was working the copper mines underneath Coniston Old Man; when Ambleside had its woollen, corn and bobbin mills, a tannery and quarries, the lakes busy with boats laden with ore, slate and woollens shipped from quay to quay and smoking bloomeries in almost every bay. Some of this industry may be seen in the old drawings but in imagination we can go back further, to the days before the trees were cut down to make charcoal for the furnaces, when the dales were choked with matted forest and undrained swamps. And even further back to Stone Age times when men were making axeheads high up in the Langdale Pikes and carrying their products over the mountains for sale to people from distant places. But this was long before the tourist 'discovered' our little corner.

Bomber's grave
༄ JULY 1968 ༄

One August night 27 years ago, a British bomber returning from a raid on Le Havre crashed in the darkness near the summit of a Lake District mountain, killing the pilot and co-pilot instantly. Miraculously, however, the three other members of the crew, hurled hundreds of feet through the air on to the mountainside, survived and one of them at least, the navigator, is still alive today. And the other day this man, a Canadian, returned to the Lake District mountains to look for the remains of his aircraft and relive those desperate moments when he faced death in the darkness on a lonely hill-top. It has not, however, been an easy mission, for the Canadian is by no means sure which mountain they hit, and his memories of their night on the fellside and their descent to the valley are vague in the extreme. Either Bowfell or Scafell, he thought, might be the mountain, but incomplete records of mountain crashes over Lakeland did not suggest either possibility. So he went up Scafell Pike and found some wreckage there – but not, he thought, the remains of their Whitley bomber. He thought they might have hit a wall on the fellside but there are no walls near the summits of either Scafell or Scafell Pike. He remembered getting down to a farm, but which one and in which valley, he has no idea. The remains of upwards of 20 aircraft still lie scattered about the fells – complete engines in some cases but elsewhere only bits of twisted metal – and more than 50 people must have met violent deaths in these disasters alone, for seven men died in one of them. It would be a long, sad pilgrimage to visit them all, but if a reader should know anything of a mountain crash in Lakeland on 23 August 1941, it might be helpful.

CHAPTER THREE

Further Afield

THE EDITOR who enlisted Harry for the *Manchester Guardian*, A.P. Wadsworth, died in harness in 1956, but his death did not mean, as so often in journalism, that his protégés were threatened by a new broom. Instead, AHG – as each of Griffin's Country Diaries was modestly signed – began a golden age. The new editor, Alastair Hetherington, was a rosy-cheeked fell-walker with a cottage in the Lake District. Harry's subjects and the mountain landscape were close to his heart and the two men became friends and walking companions.

The Diary was given more room while retaining its eminent place among the paper's grandest pieces of furniture on the leader page, and Harry also began to write occasional features and book reviews. He took pride in working for the *Manchester Guardian*, the ultimate goal of his journalist friends in Barrow and Preston days, and in the fact that his fortnightly paragraphs were treated with respect. He was understandably struck by one occasion when Hetherington phoned to apologize for a two-word cut in a diary. 'Imagine,' Harry recalled in an interview I taped with him for the *Guardian* archive in 2002. 'The editor of the *Manchester Guardian* phoning me. At home. About *two words*.' But on another occasion there had clearly been a worse sub-editing problem, because Hetherington deliberately gave the next Griffin diary a mention in that day's third leader.

Harry was into his stride, too, in the way he set about his *Guardian* work. He never kept a conventional diary nor did he make notes on his walks, which were generally some 20 miles long, or while resting on a summit after rock-climbing or down in the valley after ski runs. His only written record was his scrawled mountain log; a sort of spidery shorthand which reminded him where he had been, when and with whom – although many of the entries say 'alone'. Back at home, he wrote the Country Diary, had a break and then read the piece through and went back line by line, doing what he called 'tightening up'. He believed strongly in individual style – in his Manchester days he had bought the *Guardian* primarily to read Neville Cardus – and he paid attention to literally every word. His original typescripts are littered with fussy crossings-out, different synonyms chosen, rejected and sometimes chosen again. His cuttings books have fewer but more anguished circles, underlinings and exclamation marks for where the Manchester office had mis-set his text or, occasionally, clumsily snipped out a word or phrase. Errors wounded Harry. At the age of 93, he still instantly admitted the two occasions when readers had caught him out, once on geology and once on his references to hounds sweating through their hides, which they don't. They slaver.

Harry was an experienced man when he began the diaries in 1951. He was 40 years old and been used to the hills for almost 30 years and a skier for two decades. He knew every Lake District valley and fell. As he grew into the job, he increasingly found his

COUNTRY DIARY

THE LAKE DISTRICT: Boulders, varying in size and shape from a football to a house, are common features of mountain country and the biggest of them were given names by the Victorians. The Douglas Boulder on Ben Nevis, however, is not a boulder at all, being a considerable crag, but in the Lake District we have several and in Boulder Valley, above Coniston, a whole company of them. Most famous of all the lakeland boulders is the Bowder Stone in Borrowdale which has had to submit to the indignity of a ladder to the top and countless picture postcards, but the Pudding Stone in Boulder Valley, the Brock Stone in Kentmere, the Gash Rock in Langstrath and a few others survive in decent obscurity. Climbers know them, of course, and have put up demanding routes from which they can fall with comparative impunity, so that the Inaccessible Boulder below Low Water is far from inviolate and the Y Boulder in Mosedale even has one route that can be done feet first. Cautiously, I submit another candidate for possible nomenclature — a massive chunk of rock on the screes below Raven Crag near the Thirlmere dam. The main feature of this Raven Crag, one of the steepest in the Lake District, is a tremendous hole, perhaps 80 feet across, in the vertical face, known to climbers as The Cave, and I suggest that my rock on the screes is a boulder, not an outcrop, so that, long years ago, it fell out on the crag and left the hole. No doubt geologists could either confirm or deny this.

A. HARRY GRIFFIN.

The perfectionist: a typical page from one of Harry's cuttings books
(courtesy of Sandra Parr)

local contacts useful and many of them became characters in the Country Diaries. Wainwright, Rusty Westmoreland the climber, Geoffrey Abraham, also a climber but more famous as a mountain photographer whose classic studies of the rock faces, and men in corduroy or moleskin beetling up them, now sell in their thousands as postcards. Abraham's daughter Enid (pronounced Ennid) Wilson was an important colleague. As WJE, initials inverted for added anonymity, she joined the *Manchester Guardian* as a Country Diarist herself just before Harry, in 1950.

Anonymity, for Harry, Enid and their six colleagues was not to last. In April 1966 the *Guardian* took a small step for itself which was a vast stride for the diarists. Since Harry had joined, there had been more changes in the paper than at any time in its history. News had arrived on the front page instead of advertisements in September 1952. The venerable name of Manchester had gone from the masthead in August 1959. Above all, the byline had spread through the paper. Readers wanted to know who had written what, and most journalists enjoyed the public credit. The Country Diarists were a last refuge of anonymity and Hetherington could see no reason for them to be an exception. So at the beginning of May 1966 AHG became A.H. Griffin and A. Harry Griffin from November the following year. Almost at once, he remembered many years later with no attempt to hide the pleasure it gave him, he was stopped and questioned about the diary in Kendal's main street.

Why the A instead of Arthur? It was partly because Harry didn't like the name (any more than Harold, which also remained unused). But his daughter Sandra remembers that he was also convinced that an initial gave a man more standing in the 1950s and 1960s. His first editor was AP, the paper itself had always been the *MG*, his fellow Lakes rambler Wainwright was always A (partly through a similar dislike of his first name, Alfred). Sandra recalls her father discussing the point with a colleague called something like Fred Smith, who felt he was failing to make progress, and urging him to change subtly to Fred C. Smith. He did and was thenceforth treated with respect.

Respect was beginning to come Harry's way after 17 unbroken years of the Country Diary and it coincided with a spreading of his wings. He stepped up his features and reviews of books which came to him accompanied by a note in Palace Script typeface which started: 'The Literary Editor presents his compliments to Mr A. Harry Griffin...' Through his friendship with Hetherington, he also attended some of the *Guardian*'s big 'do's'. The paper was still a provincial ingénue in London, where its high command moved from Manchester in 1964, most other departments following in stages over the next decade. But it laid on a tremendous bash in 1972 to mark the paper's 150th anniversary and Harry was one of the guests. 'Prime ministers were two a penny,' he recalls in the taped interview in the *Guardian* archive. 'It was a very superior dinner indeed, at the Dorchester.' He remembered the German Chancellor Willi Brandt being there, the Archbishop of Canterbury, and young Jack Straw, eventually to be Home and Foreign Secretary, but then a firebrand from the National Union of Students. Harry sat between Lew Grade, as usual inseparable from a fat cigar, and the conductor of the Hallé, James Loughran – a thoughtful bit of placing. Harry had not missed a single Hallé concert during the three years, 1937–9, when he reviewed for the *Daily Mail*, and he retained a great enthusiasm. He also chatted at length to the historian A. J. P. Taylor and met the man who was to be his next editor at the *Guardian*, Peter Preston.

Harry was widening his horizons in other ways. His diary now roved more regularly afield; often to Cumbria's Howgill Fells and the Three Peaks, regularly to Scotland, and – at great strain to the family's nerves because of filing uncertainties – sometimes abroad. Here are some of those roving diaries, starting with an unusual but appealing excursion to the gentle, crag-free, most un-Griffinlike Home Counties...

Where's the scenery?
❧ NOVEMBER 1961 ❧

People in the South of England live in a smaller world than those who
inhabit, for instance, the Lake District, where I live. Their horizons
are so near and, as often as not, there is no background to the view.
The edge of the world is often not much farther away than, say, the
length of a couple of rugger fields. This is my principal reaction to a
temporary transition from the Westmorland fells to the sylvan depths
of Hertfordshire. From where I sit typing on a frosty morning, the
horizon seems only about half a mile away, whereas from almost
anywhere in Westmorland you can generally see at least ten miles.
My view on this perfect morning consists entirely of blue sky, vast,
flat, frosted lawns spattered with fallen leaves, clipped holly hedges,
and, regularly dotted across the turf and stretching to the horizon,
some of the most magnificent trees I have ever seen. Of its type it is
a superb scene but hardly a view as we know them in the North –
miles of countryside spread out below your feet or a backcloth
of rugged fells facing you across a valley. As I sit watching a grey
squirrel wriggle down a tree and scamper across the grass I wonder
whether there is anywhere in the world where one could get a
combination of the two scenes – the pastoral dignity and splendid
orderliness of a county like this and the tumbled majesty of the Lake
District. Curious how you never get quite this stillness in the fell
country – the huge trees so steady they might be painted scenery. Up
North, even on an equally glorious morning, the cloud shadows
would be chasing across the hills and there would be the movement
of flowing water, or gently waving brackens.

In the Tyrol
❧ JULY 1961 ☙

We came down from the clouds this morning, first through last night's new snow, then across the ice fall and down the rocks, and finally down grassy alps to a deep, wooded valley threaded by a foaming glacier torrent and alive with the clank of cowbells. Among the rocks we passed clumps of alpenrosen, here and there great cushions of moss campion, bright blue spikes of gentian and yellow and white flowers in profusion, but no marmots playing in and out of their little caves and, surprisingly this year, never a sight of chamois. Yesterday, from half way up a lovely, soaring snow peak we saw two eagles quartering the sky but, from the summit, nothing but hundreds of jagged peaks, piled one behind the other all round a notched horizon – white castles probing the blue heavens. We munched raisins and the traditional mint cake as we peered down on to an empty white world and then saw we were not quite alone in the mountains. Perhaps three or four thousand feet below us and two miles away, a little line of dots on the snow – Italian troops (we learned afterwards) on patrol with their rifles and machine guns. We had forgotten we were sitting on a frontier; somehow the picture looked not quite so perfect…

But today we are back in the valley with the painted wooden chalets, their terraces hung with flowers, the quaint onion-topped church, brown, muscular men at work in their tilted fields, womenfolk in national costume and everywhere the cheerful 'Grüss Gott' for the traveller down from the mountains.

Reindeer in the Cairngorms
◖ FEBRUARY 1967 ◗

It didn't seem at all strange to discover a bedraggled reindeer sheltering from the storm just inside the entrance to the chair-lift the other day, for the wind was like a knife and the ski-runs like tilted ice-rinks. Of course he might merely have come in for the company – you could see his fellows higher up on the snowbound hillside – or he might have been hoping for the chance of something more succulent than the frozen heather roots these creatures seem to live on. But he wasn't very friendly, responding to a cautious stroking by an angry swing of the head, so I left him standing disconsolate by the ticket office and looking as if he'd lost both Father Christmas and his sledge. I suppose they're harmless enough, although a notice further down the mountain warns 'Beware of Reindeer', but doesn't explain why. These were the only wild life we saw in the hills during a wild week, except for the ptarmigan in their white winter plumage hurrying through the snow, and once a handsome pheasant strutting across the track through the Rothiemurchus pines. Indeed, there were days, so fierce the winds, when these popular slopes were even deserted by the humans who normally at this time of year swarm like ants, and one day, especially, when I seemed quite alone in the mountains. Skiing that day was out of the question – you needed an ice-axe and crampons just to get across the runs – and the wind so strong on the plateau that it took you all your time to avoid being blown over the edge. But down by Lake Morlich in the late afternoon the wind suddenly dropped for half an hour, and there was the quiet splendour of purpling hills and a foreground of silvered loch with the birches and pines showing black against a golden sunset like a Chinese painting.

Discovering the Rockies
ᏺᎦ August 1974 ᎥᎦ

'The world's best view' – of the turquoise waters of Lake Louise glinting in the sunlight with the glaciers and the Snow Mountains behind – was somewhat marred by the serried ranks of parked cars and the camera-laden crowds in the foreground. All nationalities among the tourists, but mostly coach-borne Americans 'doing the Rockies'. The scenery, however, improved and the tourists thinned out – leaving only the most resolute – as we traversed the plain of the six glaciers towards Mount Victoria and we left the last of them at the first sight of the Abbot Pass. This was a day in a thousand – blue skies, crisp snow and tremendous views over a sea of peaks – and when, hours later, we returned along the lake shore the crowds had gone and the black bears had, no doubt, come out of the woods to seek out the garbage. Later that night a friendly warden took me into the woods behind the famous chateau to meet a bear he had seen an hour or two earlier but we were unlucky and saw only paw scratches on the hotel's garbage tanks. Bears are a genuine hazard in the mountains hereabouts and I was given much advice on how to cope, which didn't sound too reassuring. Another day a solo attempt on Mount Temple, the highest mountain in the area, was frustrated through heavy rain and thick mist. I got to about 10,000 feet and then decided – the mountain rescue service being an unknown quantity – to come down to Morain Lake and the spectacular Valley of the Ten Peaks. Three days in the Rockies is, of course, ridiculous. You could climb there for three months and still only scratch the surface. The Rockies have a soaring, dramatic quality not even seen in the Alps.

Down a pothole
❧ MARCH 1982 ☙

It had been 30 years since I had last been down a pothole. In those days we used carbide lamps and heavy rope ladders, wearing clothing that rarely kept us dry or warm. Today, electric headlamps, lightweight metal ladders, waterproof clothing and new safety techniques have transformed this adventurous sport which is increasingly probing the unknown magic of Britain's underground. The other day a few us spent a day at the Whernside Cave and Fell Centre in Dentdale, the headquarters for caving and potholing in this country, which has an international reputation. The highlight was the easy descent of Alum Pot, below Simon Fell, by way of Long Churn – a modest introduction to the subterranean delights of stalactites, stalagmites, fossils, almost unbelievable rock formations and caverns measureless to man. I was impressed by the quality of the instructors. They are experts in modern techniques and cave rescue but also enthusiasts, with scientific backgrounds, just as interested in underground study and the care of the environment as in exploration. Clearly, potholing is much more than climbing underground. Its adherents seem more interested in the nature and the meaning of the rock they are handling than the average climber, and there is the ever-present urge to add to human knowledge by new discoveries. Meteorological knowledge, too, is vastly important. How much rain will raise the becks and flood the caverns, at what point must one retreat? My preference will always be for mountaineering in the unlimited freedom of fresh air and sunlight, but the exploratory possibilities of caving – to tread where no one has been before – must be a wonderful incentive for the adventurous.

Valley of Ghosts
⟋ APRIL 1990 ⟍

'The Dale that Died', lonely Grisedale one thousand feet up in the hills above Garsdale, drowsed in the sleepy spring sunshine. Curlews and skylarks sang, buzzards soared, new lambs frolicked by the winding beck, celandines crowded the hedgerows and dark moors reached above green intake fields to the desolate heights of Baugh Fell. No cars, nobody about, at first sight a bright green sanctuary of rural charm, but walk a mile up the sparkling beck curving through the gritstone flags and you see that all the farmsteads, save one, lie in tumbled ruins. Look inside and note the abandoned furniture, bedding, cupboards, old radio sets, children's toys, rushes and dandelions sprouting in kitchens, sheep fleeces rotting in barns, roofs fallen in and shattered windows. This is the valley where the dalesfolk, once a happy community, gradually decided that harsh economic facts had to be faced. No longer had the upland valley, often cut-off in winter, a viable future, the little chapel had to close its doors, the people left in some cases, it seems, in a hurry for an easier life elsewhere, and lovely Grisedale, its pastures turned sour, its farm tracks overgrown, went back to Nature. Not all is quite lost; the Forestry Commission has moved in, some of the land has been let for grazing but the sadness, the tragic passing of an honest way of life, strikes you immediately. Grisedale was flooded with beauty the other afternoon but it is now a dead valley filled only with quiet despair.

Vancouver views
❧ JUNE 1991 ❧

Mostly sea and mountain here, so time has been allocated to both. The best sea day was helping to crew a 30ft sloop to the Gulf Islands and back – no wind, so cruising all the way to Pender Island for lunch, but the return, with all hands to the sheets, billowing sails and the deck at 45 degrees, an exciting chase through white-topped waves. Whistler, two hours' drive along a dramatic highway, had changed out of all recognition from the tiny cluster of shanty cabins, visited years ago, to the biggest and most brash – but many say the finest – ski development in North America. Huge hotels, restaurants and apartments compete in opulence and vulgarity, while cable cars, multiple chair lifts and tows transport thousands up the twin peaks of Whistler and Blackcomb to beautifully-laundered slopes or the sparkling powder demanded by connoisseurs. After all this high-life elegance it was almost a relief to escape the crowds and tread the lonely heights around Cypress Bowl and Hollyburn, deserted now by skiers but still carrying more snow – wonderfully skiable spring or corn snow – than the Lake District gets in a good winter. We inspected, from a respectful distance, the 2000ft of vertical and overhanging rock, on which climbers sometimes hang in hammocks for days, that makes the face of Shawamus Chief. It is an easy scramble up the back but the wall – three times the height of Pillar Rock – is terrifying merely to contemplate. And just around the corner is Shannon Falls – nearly 10 times the height, they say, of Niagara Falls. This is big country indeed.

Back on Arran
❧ JUNE 1992 ☙

First visited before the war and later, when the children were young, a frequent holiday haunt, this lovely island recently lured me again, after an absence of many years, across the sunlit waters of the firth of Clyde. Little had changed. There is still a refreshing absence of development, the roads remain unchanged and, except on Goatfell, the hills are still almost untracked – rather like Lakeland 60 years ago. In a week – again, except on Goatfell – we saw no more than a handful of people on the tops and, one day, around Beinn Tarsuinn, none at all. And, when we circumnavigated the island by car, we counted no more than half a dozen vehicles. Surprisingly, for so early in June, we encountered the midge menace – but only on warm, sunny evenings in the thickly-wooded dell outside the delightful, old manor house where we lodged in sybaritic comfort. Apart from the known delights of the heights – the soaring granite peaks, the deep-cut glens and the views across the sea to islands and the mainland hills – we especially enjoyed the splendid trees, heavy in blossom, the tropical plants and, most of all, the riot of wild flowers, everywhere. Sometimes it was almost like walking through alpine meadows in spring and, always, the golden yellow of the broom contrasting so well with the sunlit blue of the sea. More than once the unspoiled beauty of it all, without an alien feature in sight, almost took your breath away. On the right sort of day, at this time of year, Arran must surely come very close to the private picture, for some of us, of paradise. There was only one poorish day for weather. In the morning we watched about 50 seals basking on sea-washed rocks at Kildonan and, in the afternoon, did the tour of Brodick Castle and its magnificent gardens. And here I had my small moment of glory – playing, by kind invitation, a page or two of Schubert on the Bechstein grand of the late Duchess of Montrose in her opulent drawing-room at the castle, now looked after by the National Trust for Scotland.

Hail in the Dales
⮟ MAY 1994 ⮝

A sudden flurry of hail stung our cheeks as we battled, muffled up in our mountain gear, against a biting east wind to reach the summit – in late May on a modest stroll over Buckden Pike. We had hoped for a lazy day in the sunshine, spying out unfamiliar Pennine heights, but it was too cold and windy to stop, or even unfold a map, and, trying to keep our feet in the gale, we had to be content with glances at the blurred shapes of old friends like Penyghent and Ingleborough far to the west. Once you are above the limestone, always a delight to the hill walker in these friendly Yorkshire fells, you usually have to cope with the much rougher and coarser gritstone terrain, staggering through the tussocks, but on Buckden Pike the going is relatively easy and, without the east wind – and, especially, with a sight of the sun – could have been effortless. Even the bogs could be easily avoided. But there was one excuse to stop – at the prominent white memorial cross half a mile south of the summit. This commemorates five Polish airmen, flying with the RAF, who perished here, in bad weather, early in 1942. Bits of twisted wreckage from their Wellington bomber are incorporated in the memorial and there is also, below the plaque, an unexplained effigy of the head of a fox. Apparently there was one survivor from the terrible crash – an airman who, with two broken legs, managed to drag himself two miles down the hillside to Starbotton, crawling on his hands and knees, by following the tracks of a fox in the snow. Thus an unknown animal has achieved a measure of fame for 50 years now. We completed our round by following a section of the Dales Way along the winding Wharfe from Starbotton, back to

Buckden – interesting enough but, judging from the map, probably not as rewarding as the even more winding section from Kettlewell. We had driven into Wharfedale by turning right at Hawes and climbing south along the interesting moorland road that, above Oughtershaw, reaches a height of 1,929 feet – more than 400 feet higher than Kirkstone Pass and only 40 feet lower than Black Combe. I know of roads in Scotland that are higher than this but, discounting the private road to Great Dun Fell that reaches 2,780 feet, there can't be many in England. The Yorkshire Dales which I only know intimately in their western, limestone section always impress with their beautiful stone villages, the neatness of meadows and woodlands and the spaciousness of the heights with their vast, spreading moorlands and their towering cloudscapes.

High Cup Nick
❧ OCTOBER 1995 ❧

One of the books in my mountain library describes the great ravine of High Cup Nick as 'one of the wonders of the British Isles', yet few of my friends have ever seen it and most have no idea where it is. It lies about five miles north-east of Appleby and you get a splendid view of it motoring over Orton Moor to the county town – a great, saucer-shaped crater a few miles to the south of Cross Fell and the huge white 'golf ball' on Great Dun Fell that was gouged out of the northern Pennines at the end of the Ice Age. I had explored it several times, and even scrambled on some of the ricketty pinnacles – but not for at least 40 years. So on a recent bright October morning, with needle-sharp visibility in every direction, two of us went to have a look at the place to refresh my memory. The approach from the lovely village of Dufton along a section of the Pennine Way, into quite a biting east wind, was easy and straightforward, so that in an hour or so we were in sight of the bite into the fells which must be about two miles deep. Some of the pinnacles are interesting – a local cobbler is said to have soled a pair of shoes on the tiny, airy summit of one of them. But one of the most remarkable features is the stone wall that seems to climb almost vertically up the side of the gorge for nearly 1000ft – a fitting monument to the men who built it hundreds of years ago. Just beyond the Nick is Maize Beck, marked 'Danger Area' on the map, where two walkers died many years ago, trying to cross in flood conditions, the body of one of them being swept downstream for ten or twelve miles and finishing up trapped among boulders at the top of High Force. Notices now warn of the danger and draw attention to an important footbridge. One of the delights of visits to these northern hills is the return in late afternoon or early evening straight into the westering sun; most of the Lakeland hills, from Wild Boar Fell to the buttresses of Blencathra, stretched – a progression of pinnacles – along the horizon.

The empty Cheviots
ꙮ OCTOBER 1997 ꙮ

My apologies to my fellow Country Diarist Veronica Heath for trespassing into her territory, and my shame at having to admit that this was my very first visit. I had been to the Himalayas and the Rockies and many other high places but never just next door to the Northumberland National Park. I will certainly go again for, compared with my over-crowded, tourist-ridden Lake District, these swelling uplands seemed refreshingly unspoiled and almost completely free from traffic. We hardly met another car within the national park and on the hills, instead of stumbling along stony tracks, trod easily along grassy paths – rather like the Lakeland I remember 70 years ago. The impression I retain of this splendid national park is of broad acres uplifted high – more extensive even than Yorkshire's – sweeping to far horizons with vast skyscapes, and, always away to the north-west, the switchback shape of the Cheviot Hills. Just underneath the Cheviot itself, in wild goat country, we had the long length of the lovely Harthope Burn completely to ourselves and only on Windy Gyle, the summit that just probes into Scotland, did we see other people. You drive along the picturesque Coquet valley, past prosperous-looking farmlands, tramp easily up pleasantly-winding tracks, hop over a stile to a trig point, and there, 2000ft below your boots, are the Scottish Lowlands. We did some of the tourist things as well – Hadrian's Wall, Kielder Water, Holy Island and the splendours of Cragside and its thickly-wooded acres. And we breakfasted royally each day in what had been the shippon of a tastefully converted farmhouse looking down on Rothbury, through morning mist from the lower slopes of the Simonside Hills. But, mostly, my memories are of my first sighting of the long blue line of the Cheviot Hills and then of our stroll along some of these almost-untracked tops with different countries on either side and not a building to be seen.

The Howgill caterpillars
☙ AUGUST 1999 ❧

The northern half of the delectable Howgill Fells – beyond the Yorkshire Dales national park – is one of the loneliest, but most rewarding, hill areas in the country. During a modest round last week of three fells around the 2000ft contour, we saw nobody all day, not even in the distance, although the traffic was streaming, almost bumper to bumper, along the A685 a couple of miles away. We started from the scattered hamlet of Weasdale where, 40 years ago, I bought the young trees for the garden of my previous home, just inside the Lake District National Park. The nurseries, at around 800 feet above sea-level, are said to be the highest in the country, so I was sure the trees would flourish in my rather exposed, east-facing garden on the 500 foot contour. And so they did.

A minor reason for our recent trip was to look for caterpillars. One day in May last year, while having our sandwiches near the summit of Green Bell, we found, to our alarm, we were sitting among thousands, probably millions, of green caterpillar-like creatures – so many you could squash dozens at every step. And, a couple of hundred yards away, there were thousands of seagulls eating them – a cloud of white on the fellside that had puzzled us as we climbed the hill. Apparently the caterpillars were eating the fell grass, at an unbelievable rate, and the farmers were naturally concerned. But last week the grass looked as lush as usual and, despite a lengthy search over a wide area, we couldn't find a single caterpillar. Either they'd been exterminated or had gone elsewhere.

From Randygill Top, Green Bell and Hooksey we saw breathtaking views that made our day – the blue shapes of the Lakeland fells, from Coniston to the 'back o' Skiddaw', strung along the horizon; close at hand, to the east and south, the sunlit ramparts of Wild Boar and the Yorkshire peaks; and, to the north, the bright green pastures of the Lune valley, with its farms, tarns and woodlands, and the whole, wide, wonderful sweep of old Westmorland.

Limestone highway
OCTOBER 2000

Traversing a sort of shelf on the soaring flank of Mallerstang Edge, hundreds of feet above the highest railway in England, is a remarkable track marked on the maps as, simply, the High Way.

This rough track, in places a limestone 'pavement', crossing becks and waterfalls and snaking round potholes, is the route the formidable Lady Anne Clifford, one of the most powerful women in the country and the owner of at least six castles, used to travel in her carriage in the seventeenth century. Frequently, inspecting her properties, she had to go from Skipton Castle to Pendragon Castle. These must have been exciting journeys but uncomfortable. The other day, between the showers, we walked a couple of miles along the High Way to catch the flavour of her journeys.

About a mile north of the county boundary where the High Way dips down to the winding River Eden and the long length of Mallerstang stretches out to the distant hills, we came upon a curious structure. This was a modern 'sculpture', not offensive like the monstrous windmills on Lambrigg Fell but nevertheless a strange erection. It consists of two slabs of dressed limestone, about nine feet high, so arranged that the space between them might be thought to resemble the winding Eden far below. I understand there are ten of these 'sculptures' by different artists, marking the length of the river – a concept that may well appeal to many people, although I prefer my hills without adornment.

Grass tracks
≈ MAY 2002 ≈

Since I first explored them just after the war, carrying my skis and looking for snow slopes, the Howgill Fells have always entranced me. Compared with Lakeland, overrun by the hordes and vastly over-publicized, they have retained their quiet, unspoiled beauty. You never see crowds in the Howgills, nor litter. The other day, sunny with a fresh wind, on a bracing walk to Arant Haw (1989ft), just visible as a shapely cone from the back of my house, we saw only one person all day – a man with a Border Collie just like my Sambo, staunch companion on scores of mountains.

The views from the summit were quite outstanding – close up, the highest of the Howgills, a long row of rounded tops, rather like mud pies, and, far off, all the Yorkshire heights with the Lakeland fells crowding the horizon. The going throughout was on the sort of grassy, velvety tracks we used to enjoy in Lakeland before they were worn away but, to a nonagenarian, quite steep at times.

I remembered my first visit to Arant Haw more than 50 years ago when my brother and I, using two parked cars, walked from Tebay to Sedbergh, collecting all the summits on the way. The last ones, before the final trot down into the town, were Arant Haw and Winder, up which the boys of Sedbergh School used to climb before breakfast. Because of their proximity, their unspoiled charm and their comfort to ageing feet, these lovely Howgill hills might well become my last, some day, and I couldn't wish a more delightful place for my final wanderings. I would be looking out at my beloved Lakeland fells but cleverly avoiding their stony tracks.

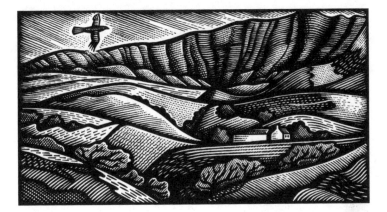

CHAPTER FOUR

Crag Rat, Coniston Tiger

THE MOST STRIKING photographs of Harry Griffin are those in which he is clinging to a rock wall like a spider with a beaky nose and moustache, a hemp rope trailing away from his shoulder into the abyss. He was at his most exhilarated and passionate when scaling the crags of the Lake District or their spikier counterparts in Scotland, and on one occasion in the Himalayas, where he came closer than anywhere else to losing his life.

His passion for climbing turned some Country Diaries literally into cliffhangers. All the others were influenced by the friends he made through the sport. These included Oxbridge professors, Lancashire grocers and a typewriter salesman from Vienna, Walter Ingham, who met Harry on a bus in Preston in the early 1930s and was always trying to enlist him in money-making schemes. They nearly started a chain of circulating libraries but, not at all to Harry's surprise, Ingham, who rose to the rank of major during the

Second World War, eventually made a fortune by founding one of Britain's biggest winter-sporting firms. He invited the Griffins on holiday in the 1950s, when Harry remembers a lissom young woman courier breathing in admiration: 'You mean, you actually *know* the Major?' On the rock face, this hugely varied group of enthusiasts were resolutely equals – mates and 'tigers', a term from slang for high-altitude porters used during mountaineers' assaults on Kangchenjunga in the Himalayas.

Climbing began for Harry in Barrow library, when he moved from Shackleton's *South* to the Fell and Rock Club journals on the next shelf. Flicking through them, he was enthralled and knew that this was what he most wanted to do. A familiar local name kept recurring in the journals: George Basterfield, the town's mayor. So off went Harry to Barrow town hall – then as now a most impressive building – where he asked to see the mayor. What might a callow 17-year-old want? enquired the janitor, an imposing official straight out of a Stanley Holloway rhyme. 'I want to ask him where I can get my boots nailed for climbing,' said Harry. 'That'll be alright then, in you go,' said the janitor, who knew his Basterfield. Although Harry thought the mayor looked disappointingly unlike a climber with his bald head, glasses and stout girth, he had gone to the right man.

Basterfield told Harry to go and see Coniston's cobbler, George Stevens, behind the Black Bull in the village, tell him George Basterfield had recommended him, and all would be fixed. So it was; but not only that. The mayor invited the boy to meet him the following week at Torver on the Coniston Road for some climbs on the adjacent, famous Dow (pronounced Doe) Cragg. Together they tramped up a muddy track where Harry's love of the hills was sealed. Basterfield showed him the difference between white-faced Herdwick sheep and 'Swardels', the Swaledale breed from Yorkshire, and pointed out lines of copper and wrinkles of garnet in the rocks – wonders Harry had never understood in dry geography

COUNTRY DIARY (for use on MONDAY . JULY 29th)

~~tapping from~~
for ~~translation~~
THE LAKE DISTRICT :   Two hours seemed a satisfying time ~~forcing~~ for ~~xxSxkkx~~

the ascent of Great Gable, ~~without stops~~ , from Honister Pass by a slightly

geriatric octogenarian, accompanied by a non-mountaineering ~~xxpxixi~~ *friend* companion .

The descent , by Windy Gap, Stone Cove and Moses' Trod, took a little longer

since zealously-shepherded ~~~~ *Rolly*
~~but~~ we were delayed by school parties and Boy Scouts on the upper reaches and
lake
byphotography when the Buttermere lakes and tarns ,flooded in sunlight, and the

bold upthrust of Pillar Rock almost cried out to be noticed. Many years ago ,

making
when ~~I would have made~~ a quicker round , I remember writing ~~thinking~~ —not then
would be
knowing anything about it —that this ~~xxx/~~the best way up Gable for octogenarians
more stony
; now I know that it is . But the route is getting rougher and ~~xxxxxx~~ every

year —and therefore more tiring — and , although we made huge sweeps to seek
was
out grassier ways , it ~~is~~ impossible to avoid most of the stones. It was a
racing *giving*
beautiful, ~~warm,day~~ sunny day with/cloud shadows ~~providing~~ changing pictures of

these loveliest of fells but there was thick mist on top and not even much of a
sight
view from the Westmorland Cairn . I had hoped for a ~~view~~ of climbers on the

superb swwep of Engineers Slabs but Gable Crag ~~xxxxxxxxxx~~ a curiously-neglected

climbingground nowadays , was deserted. Later , however , from a perch on the
in the afternoon sunlight ,
Fleetwith Pike quarry road , we watched an ascent/of Honister Wall , just across
seemed
the top,of the pass . We saw walkers on what ~~xxxxx~~ a new track from Moses' Trod
chosen
to Haystacks and wondered whether these were pilgrims to Wainwright's ~~favourite~~,
n
~~Inominate Tarn~~ resting place - Inominate Tarn . The *H*onister car-park had been
encountered —*including elderly folk on slope*
full and we must have ~~xxxx~~ a hundred people on and around the summit of Gable~~xx~~
——
—on a weekday . After Helvellyn and Scafell Pike, the latter because of its
— *rightly* *the*
height distinction, Great Gable must,be ~~xxx~~ most favoured mountain , ~~and right~~,
~~so~~ —and , by our route , one of the easiest.

*An original typescript: Harry meticulously cut his paper to suit
the number of words the* Guardian *required*
(courtesy of Sandra Parr)

lessons. Then he stopped and peered at marks in the mud. 'Ah, we're going to have Hargreave and Clegg on the crag with us today,' he said. He had recognized the presence of the pair – A.T. Hargreave and Billy Clegg, who were two of the best climbers in Britain – by the pattern of their nails.

In the event, the pair spent the whole day with Basterfield and his apprentice, spinning yarns between climbs about their mountain 'gang', the Yewdale Vagabonds, whose motto was 'Every cliff will yield to the power of Basterfield.' Harry never looked back. He was soon a founder-member of the Coniston Tigers, a posse of Lakeland lads who bought a timber garage in Barrow and reassembled it at Coniston as the base for years of hair-raising climbs by a new generation of vagabonds. This was Harry's apprenticeship as a 'crag rat', a less grand but apt alternative to 'tiger', which he often used in the Country Diaries. He got to know the climbers' grubby cave base at the foot of Dow as well as his own kitchen, as he slid up and down hairline cracks in true rodent fashion.

Climbing also brought other great advantages to the young man who had left Barrow municipal secondary school with buckets of enthusiasm but formal qualifications limited to six credits in English Literature, History, French, Maths, Physics-with-Chemistry and Art. Among the madcap guests at the Wastwater Hotel, daring one another to do strange feats like the 'billiard table traverse' which he mentions in one of the diaries, were university men who were the leading experts in their field. They never stopped talking, Harry often recalled, except when they were singing unsuitable songs, with a Regius professor from Oxford beating out the time with the fire tongs. One climbed blindfold for bets. Another, the poet George Winthrop Young, had a special attachment on his artificial leg to enable him to cling to holds. Harry sat at their feet, utterly absorbed. This was his 'university of life' where he also learned the skills of argument and debate which were to serve him well on committees and campaigning groups later on.

Climbing also honed his eye for a character, whether it was Basterfield combining his rock face outings with delivering oranges and grapefruits to customers, or the self-styled Professor of Adventure, Millican Dalton, constructing a raft to commute between his hut on a crag above Derwentwater and Keswick market. They were all to appear in the Country Diaries, along with accounts of scrambles and ascents, not just in the Lakes, but on the Scottish mountains, in the Alps and once, terrifyingly, in the Himalayas.

During his only visit to the world's greatest mountain range, on leave from the 14th Army's headquarters, Harry rashly set out alone across a steep, snow-covered slope, kicking footholds as he went. As he contoured along, the snow began to harden and gradually turn into ice. Without an axe, further progress was impossible and he finally decided to turn back – a very delicate manoeuvre. As he twisted round, easing one leg sideways and swivelling on the other heel, he slipped, fell and slid, faster and faster, over the ice towards the rim of the precipice below. At the last moment, spotting a rock outcrop, he kicked himself sideways, grabbed for the rock, caught hold of it and saved his life.

Harry had many other adventures and saw many friends come to grief, including Basterfield who lost a thumb after a careless belay. His companion fell and the hemp rope simply sliced the thumb off. But Harry avoided such horrors. The closest he came was on the Migraine route in Deepdale where the whole rockface suddenly started to move. By jamming his knee forward he held it for a vital moment as his second jumped clear. Then tonnes of rock crashed down and, as Harry laconically notes in *The Coniston Tigers*, 'the route now goes to the left'.

Chimney tree

ᐰᐰ DECEMBER 1953 ᐰᐰ

Sixty years ago, a young man leading the ascent of the first rock climb in this valley used for a foothold to get into a lower chimney the exposed, withered root of an ancient holly tree, projecting, fed by some hidden soil, out of the vertical rock. As his weight came on the twist of dying fibre it sagged but did not snap and the climber was able to reach his holds above. The other day we happened to be repeating the same climb and, like everyone before us, used the same old root, now scratched down to finger thickness. A trifling incident, perhaps, but the next day I was chatting to the old pioneer himself and his first question was: 'Is the old root still there?' How pleasant to be able to tell him that it was, that it still creaked ominously, but that it had withstood sixty years of use and seemed likely to remain there for ever.

The old man, thinking back over a lifetime's memories, asked whether we had noticed the old track underneath the crags where as boys they had found old coins, perhaps dropped by smugglers creeping by night across the steep fellside. Had we seen the stone – whitewashed annually at one time – marking the place where, nearly 240 years ago, a young lady of noble birth scrambled up the crag in her flight to London to plead unavailingly for the life of her soldier husband? Yes, we had seen these things, as well as the bright new buds, the raven's nest, and the centuries-old fireplaces, open to the sky, in the farm down the valley.

The rat cave
❧ MAY 1960 ☙

To the cave-dweller a tent is an affectation and a caravan or hut a senseless luxury. A cave, they say, is cheaper, handier for the job in hand, and much more comfortable. Besides, it does not need lugging up the fellside. The caves are underneath the crags and are used by the younger and more single-minded climbers. 'Crag rats' they are called – these wild, young acrobats – by the superior and secretly envious. Few people could find their way to these caves for there are no tracks to the entrances and, for the most part, the bearded adventurers keep their litter under control. The caves, generally underneath a jumble of giant boulders, are paved with turf or bracken with gaps in the walls filled with moss or smaller boulders to keep out the wind. For pallet, one of them has a piece of aeroplane fuselage found higher up the fellside; others have beds of straw or heather. Inside, you may find a petrol stove and a store of food. These are the places where the crag rats spend their weekends – only five minutes away from the foot of the climbs. They sleep, as well as you or I, in down-filled sleeping bags and, as like as not, have a morning dip in the tarn before their bacon and eggs. Shopping in the villages, they look unkempt and scruffy, but they are immensely fit. The worst of them may be rough and unmannerly; the best are genuine lovers of the open air, young men at peace with the hills.

An anxious moment
❧ JUNE 1965 ☙

The climber returning to the crags after a lengthy absence may not find it easy. There may still be the well-remembered feel of rough rock and the exhilaration of neat, unhurried progress, but the confidence to step up on tiny holds in the expectation of better ones to come and the happy disregard of steepness and exposure may well be lacking. Two of us discovered this truism one bright afternoon recently on a very familiar crag and found ourselves sneaking off to claw our way clumsily up a modest route that a year or two ago we might have used for an easy way off but hardly as a worthwhile climb. At the top, nerves jangled, muscles tensed, and breath a little laboured, we decided to call it a day – and get into training before our next expedition. Perhaps as a sop to our wounded pride we decided to walk over the hill into the next valley instead of running down the to the road, and some time later were watching two youngsters half our age high up among the overhangs of a great cliff on a dramatic new route. The rope hung down in mid-air, feet out from the face, and the climbers were clinging to the sketchiest of holds, but there was no alarm or even doubt in their reactions. 'It's a bit thin, that move,' we heard the leader shout down to his second, 'but there's a good hand-jam a little higher up. Take your time.' The appalling verticality made our climb look like a staircase and we felt a little envious of their youth, their courage, their relish of severity and their contempt for danger. Sadly, we shouldered the old rope and slunk down through the bracken and the long shadows for a reviving drink. How wonderful, we thought, to be young and fit and in the hills on such a lovely day.

Napes Needle
༄ MARCH 1966 ༄

The most famous bit of rock in England is Napes Needle, perched high up among the ridges on the side of Great Gable and looking down on the patchwork fields of Wasdale Head nearly 2000ft below. It was first climbed 80 years ago by W.P. Haskett Smith, a young Oxford graduate who was later to be revered as the 'father' of climbing, and its ascent was the first significant landmark in the development of the new sport of rock-climbing. Haskett Smith climbed it alone, leaving his fell-pole at the foot, and left his handkerchief jammed in a crevice on the top block to prove it. Fifty years later, at the age of 74, but roped this time between two other distinguished climbers, he went up again and, seated on the top block, made the extempore remark that has since passed into history. 'Tell us a story,' shouted someone from the admiring crowds below, and the old man, never at a loss for words, replied on the instant: 'There is no other story. This is the top storey.'

Since the first ascent, all sorts of indignities have been heaped upon the old Needle. It has been climbed thousands of times by at least eight routes, small boys and girls have been hauled up, stunt climbs and speed record attempts have been perpetrated on its smooth walls, and it has been photographed, sketched, filmed and televised. People have lit fires on top, stood on their heads, eaten meals and danced jigs, and if there are three of you on the edge of the top block, you can gently rock it. I know; I've done it. But the other day, the Needle looked none the worse for its harsh treatment, except that the holds are lightly polished here and there.

Pillar Rock
AUGUST 1968

There's a couple of hours' walking from anywhere to get to Pillar Rock, which makes it a different sort of climbing centre than these 'modern' crags within handy reach of main roads and hotel bars. Climbers met on the rock, therefore, tend to be determined devotees quite prepared to walk up mountains to find their cliffs, rather than singleminded gymnasts for whom an urban quarry face would serve equally well. They were also likely to be much thinner on the ground and the other day, with the crags in superb condition, there were only six people beside myself on the biggest lump of rock in England. The walk from Buttermere in August can be long and hot but the steep scramble up from the Liza and the massed conifers was made enjoyable by the sight of the heather in bloom and the refreshing taste of the bilberries which grow here-abouts in great profusion. The real lodestone of this walk is always the sight, high up and straight ahead, of the great bulk of the Rock – rather like two cathedrals piled on top of each other, but bigger than any cathedral in the world. I reached the top of the Rock by a route befitting a lone and slightly decrepit climber and joined the others in leisurely contemplation of the scenery. Strings of walkers looking, from High Man, like moving matchsticks were crossing the rooftree of Pillar Mountain but there was no other movement, save for the clouds, over the whole tumbled landscape. No sound, either, with the becks stilled by the long, dry summer – not even a slither of scree from sliding sheep on the fellside far below. Westwards towards the lake, the sea and the sunset stretched the dark carpet of conifers and northwards rose the blue evening hills around Buttermere as we smoked in silence on our steeple top, oblivious of the busy world so far away.

Brief encounter
❧ DECEMBER 1973 ❦

The neatly-kicked footholes in the snow crept up the side of Red Screes like a ladder until they disappeared into swirling mists. Somebody was ahead of me but I couldn't see or hear him – just the steepening snows rearing up into the greyness and the sound of the wind roaring round the corrie and bouncing off the black cliffs. The footholes were precise and firm and just where I would have placed them so that it was a comfortable ladder except where black ice glazed the rocks. I could see where my unseen leader had taken his ice-axe off his rucksack and started to use it – at the foot of a steep little wall of snow just below the entrance to the corrie. From this point onwards there was a regular progression of holes pierced by the shaft and here and there a scraped foothole. My original intention had been to cross the corrie and climb slantwise up the ridge but the other man had chosen the gully straight ahead so I followed his trail and soon emerged, in a buffeting gale and a flurry of new snow, on the crest. Visibility was less than five yards but there was no need for a compass bearing to find the summit for the toeholes were now footprints and I could even estimate his size. A big man I thought, wearing newish boots, about size ten. Reaching the ice-plastered cairn a few moments later, I found him just ready to leave – yes, a big man, shrouded up to the eyes against the cold and wind, dimly seen in the whiteout like a wraith. It was no place for conversation for the wind was deafening and the cold intense. 'Bit rough,' was my contribution, and his, 'I'll be glad to be down' and we went our separate ways, disappearing immediately into the darkening greyness.

A hidden gem
⟣ MAY 1974 ⟢

Little-known delectable places in the hills should not be advertised lest they be overrun by the hordes. And this is hardly selfish for anybody can discover their own 'secret' places. Several times I have revealed the location of hidden pools, natural rock gardens or unfamiliar crags only to regret my ingenuousness later. One of the worst examples was my gift, some time ago, of a necklace of glorious pools in a little-visited valley where, until recently, I had never seen a soul; at Easter the place looked like a section of Blackpool beach. The other day three of us discovered a 'new' and exhilarating way up a Lake District mountain but this time, apart from revealing that the ridge is in the Eastern fells, we will keep it to ourselves. I had spotted the craggy ridge a week earlier when, seen against the setting sun, it looked like something in the Dolomites – a bold staircase of dark, rock towers. In reality it was not as dramatic as this but at least it gave a thousand feet of scrambling and was protected, at its base, by a 10ft high rock wall that only fell at the third attempt. Perhaps other people have been this way before but there were no scratches, footprints, orange peel or beer-can rings and the place, which is much more rewarding and far steeper than any of the Lake District edges, is not mentioned in any guide book. A good place, we thought, for retired rock climbers or adventurous youngsters – a natural route, straight to the summit, which, for some reason, seems to have been missed by all but the ravens. There is a tiny tarn near the top and here we ate our sandwiches, well content with the view of Pillar and the Scafells and our new – or at least unfamiliar – staircase to the heights.

Twin Pillars
↷ November 1977 ↶

So still and quiet on top of Pillar Rock the other day you could use unshielded matches and hear the murmur of the becks nearly 2000ft below. And yet, an hour later, on the higher summit of Pillar, the mountain, we could hardly stand against the south-westerly gale and barely converse without shouting. The gale presumably had been blowing all afternoon but the Rock, sheltered by the mountain wall, was a haven of quietude on a wild day of scurrying cloud on the highest tops and spraying becks in the dales. Not a good day for climbing with greasy rocks but, once on top of the Rock, we could sprawl at our ease, look down the dark conifer carpet to the lake and the sea, see the upper crags in Birkness Combe across the dale lighted by a shaft of sunlight and count the tarns on Haystacks. Reaching the whaleback summit of Pillar was a double exhilaration – first, after the stillness, the buffeting gale, and second, the fantastic skyscape. The sea and the Wasdale hills were blotted out by a gigantic curtain of ink-black cloud, topped by a level blanket of white cotton wool. And this blanket, lighted from above by the westering sun, glowed with fire – a rim of gold beneath the blue vault of the sky. In a few moments we were enveloped in cloud and trotted down to the valley in clammy greyness and gathering dark, but we had had our brief reward. And later, splashing down flooded tracks to Wasdale Head, we had our second reward – a full moon, huge and shining, peeping over the shoulder of Great End and lighting our way, through familiar evening smells and sounds of woodsmoke and falling waters, to the lights of the inn.

The devils' hill
SEPTEMBER 1980

With more than a dozen ways up, some still untracked, it is difficult to tire of Blencathra, 'the hill of devils'. By adding variations you could probably permute ascents and descents to give a different round each week of the year – and discover something new each time. A recent round, on a sunny, blustery day, took me on a scrambling route up the southern wall of Sharp Edge, above the tarn, and down the ravine of Doddick Gill, after a tour of the summit ridge and surrounding tops. All the south- or east-facing buttresses of Blencathra are rewarding for ascent or descent – especially in winter – and the gills between these spurs are wonderful places for a bit of mild adventuring. The purist should climb or attempt all the waterfalls and water slides, and then find a rock route to the summit or to one of the containing ridges. On the way he will be impressed by the agility and sure-footedness of mountain sheep, grazing on the terraces among the crags and looking, from a distance, rather like the kittiwakes perched on the ledges of St Bees Head. Bilberries grow in profusion in some of the steepest places but, unless you time your visit with exactitude, will have already been cropped by these four-footed mountaineers. These splendid ravines – flooded with sunlight on good days and full of the music of falling waters – are easy to enter but rarely visited, perhaps because the ridges are so popular. Norman Nicholson [Cumbria's best-known 20th-century poet] once wrote that Blencathra, hollowed out, would fit over London, and that all the people alive on earth could easily be heaped inside – a rather difficult theory to check. But, certainly, this is one of our biggest mountains in area – and one of the most varied and enjoyable.

Climbing a billiard table
NOVEMBER 1997

Nearly 70 years after my first visit, I went back to the old inn at Wasdale Head, where the British sport of rock-climbing was born. Much had changed. The entrance hall was no longer heaped with dozens of pairs of heavily-nailed climbing boots, shiny with dubbin, and the old hat-stand no longer garlanded with climbing ropes and long-handled ice-axes. Just beyond the hall, in my earlier visits, was the smoke-room where, after dinner, I would sit at the feet of the great men – several of them university professors but, all of them, climbers, and, some of them, quite famous climbers. first, they would tell stories – wild, funny tales of adventures or near disasters on icy peaks or overhanging rocks – and, then, almost unbelievably, they would start singing, and one of them, a lawyer, a doctor or an austere company chairman, would seize the fire-irons and, banging on anything to hand, noisily beat out the rhythm. Beyond the smoke-room was the billiards room – never used for billiards but, instead, for a dangerous game called billiards-fives, or for strange feats of strength and agility that often involved a traverse of the table, with your feet on the walls of the room. These rather dingy corners for the unleashing of youthful high spirits have now been transformed into elegant drawing rooms, appropriate for afternoon tea or a little Mendelssohn on the piano. On the landing, I remember, there was a huge oak chest, full of old socks, knee-breeches, sweaters, jackets – anything at all to replace lost, forgotten or hopelessly-torn clothes. It's all gone now and nobody knows where. But the stable door traverse in the yard, up which we used to climb into the upper door, is still there – and still painted 'Post horses' – and I was delighted to find that the tiny garden, crammed with mountain plants brought down from the fells by my very first climbing leader, remains in a corner of the car park. Wonderful memories of happier days.

Scrambling with ghosts
～ JULY 1999 ～

Exactly 70 years ago I started rock-climbing on Dow Crag near Coniston and it is now 10 years since my last climbs on Grey Crag, Buttermere – 60 years of careful and immensely satisfying progress up rock walls, gullies and cracks, and a lifetime of stimulating excitement and adventure. But climbing is only one part of mountaineering and, in the wider aspect of our appreciation of the great outdoors, perhaps only a small part. With age we realise it is the whole mountain or hill and its relationship with surrounding features that really matters.

The other day, with a sunny weather forecast, we went up Bowscale Fell from the lovely hamlet of Mungrisdale and on top encountered headwinds that stopped us in our tracks, thick cloud above 2000ft and relentless, soaking drizzle. Bowscale and its neighbours are undemanding hills but their traverse, under these conditions, gave almost as much satisfaction as the completion of an awkward climb. Before the clouds blotted out the views there was the peep, 800 feet below our feet, of the black pool of Bowscale Tarn, with its Victorian legend of two undying fish – one of our finest mountain tarns but seldom visited nowadays. A couple of miles north across the valley of the Caldew rose the bulk of the remarkable Carrock Fell with the remains of the early British hill fort plain to see on the summit. Another sighting, on the way up, was the unusual, sideways view of Sharp Edge on Blencathra close enough, on a clear day, for one to pick out people scrambling along it. Bowscale Fell starts with a steepish scramble through gorse bushes but thereafter, around the Bannerdale horseshoe, is a delightfully easy stroll on heather and bilberry. To your left, as you mount the contours, is the long ridge of Souther Fell, where, on Midsummer Day 1745, 26 witnesses attested on oath they had seen troops, horses and gun-carriages marching across the fell – a supernatural mystery that has never been solved.

View from a ledge
❧ SEPTEMBER 1999 ☙

From a rock ledge about 600ft up the south-facing slopes of Loughrigg there is a surprise view of the long length of Windermere flanked, on one side, by the soaring sweep of Wansfell and, on the other, by the wooded uplands of Claife Heights. The upper reaches of the lake will probably be dotted with the white sails of small craft, like butterflies becalmed on a pond and now and again a speed boat, trailing its white wake, might swoop across the water. A few hundred feet below your airy perch are the splendid gardens, woodlands and lawns of White Craggs, and looking round you may peep into many quiet corners of the surrounding dales.

For many years, on sunny summer evenings, after dinner in their home at the foot of the slope, an elderly man and his wife would walk up to this rock ledge, a steepish stroll of 10 minutes or so, and quietly admire the lovely, familiar scene. Then they would walk back home through the woods. Recently, after the expenditure of a considerable amount of energy – for all ways round here are steep and stony – a splendid wooden seat was installed on the ledge, in memory of this remarkable man. The inscription, beautifully carved into the teak, reads: 'Sid Cross (1913–98). A true Westermerian who loved his Langdale.'

He was one of my oldest and closest friends, for we first met on the crags almost 70 years ago. Sid was a brilliant rock climber, and he and his wife, Jammie, were for many years the popular hosts at the Old Dungeon Ghyll Hotel in Langdale, which they transformed into the mountaineering centre of the Lake District. More than that, Sid was the driving force behind the formation of the Langdale mountain rescue team, for which service he was appointed MBE.

Appropriately, it was his old friends from mountain rescue who organized the memorial seat, so that others could share with Sid and Jammie the wonderful view they never tired of admiring. Fit it into a traverse of Loughrigg, the queen of the lesser heights of Lakeland, some time.

Veteran tigers

❧ OCTOBER 1999 ☙

After a thorough grounding on the Lakeland fells as a teenager, I started rock climbing just over 70 years ago and two years later nine of us formed the Coniston Tigers, a tiny unofficial climbing group with our own rough hut on the shore of Coniston Water. Here, for many years before and after the Second World War, we spent our weekends, using the hut as our base for the climbs on

Dow Crag, Gimmer Crag in Langdale or the Wasdale crags, and every year we went north to the Scottish snows.

Sadly, only four of the original nine are still alive today but three of these managed to get along to the launch of my mountain autobiography, *The Coniston Tigers*, in Kendal recently, our ages varying from a youthful 87 to a determined 90 years. Also present was a sprightly old gentleman who, at 98, is probably the oldest member of the senior climbing club to which I have belonged for most of my lifetime. Regrettably, mountaineering has claimed many young lives but, happily, it also often seems to go hand in hand with longevity. I remember bumping into the old gent in the street a year or two ago when he told me he was 96 that day. 'And,' he added, with enthusiasm, 'I can remember every minute of a day 75 years ago when we went up the Finsterarhorn.'

The book launch took place at the Kendal Mountain Film Festival where desperate deeds on vertical rock or ice in many parts of the world were portrayed on cinema screens – in striking contrast to my own far more modest potterings. Strangely, the weekend was one of the most splendid for months – dawn to dusk sunshine, clear skies and invigorating breezes – so we had the anomaly of hundreds of keen mountain folk condemned to sit in dark cinemas – having paid in advance – when the Lakeland fells and crags were beckoning more urgently than they had done for some time.

An adventurous vicar

❧ OCTOBER 2000 ☙

The most secret and least known memorial in the Lakeland fells may well be the one commemorating the Revd James Jackson, an adventurous clergyman who climbed Pillar Rock at 80 and died in a fall near the Rock in 1878, at the age of 82, making another attempt. This is certainly the view of a friend of mine, John Wilson, a retired police officer living near Ulverston who devotes much of his time to tracking down old cairns, memorials, inscriptions and other curiosities in the fells.

I have long known of the memorial to 'Steeple' Jackson – he once climbed his church steeple to repair a weather vane – and when I was regularly climbing on Pillar Rock I often searched Great Doup, the wild combe just east of the rock where he fell, but never found it. But now John tells me he found it sometime ago, after a long search, and has sent me a photo of it – a simple cross, about 18in high and 9in in width, professionally carved in the face of a crag high up in Great Doup.

Old records show that two years after his death, mountain friends placed a cairn and iron cross on the spot but on 16 August 1906 other friends undertook a more permanent memorial. Three distinguished mountaineers of the day arranged for a Cockermouth marble mason, Benson Walker, to have the memorial carved near where the body was found.

If you're fit and used to places like this, then have a look for it some time, but take care. It's very steep and rough up there and, at this time of the year, usually wet and slippery.

Falcon's nest
⌘ AUGUST 2003 ⌘

Climbing on Dow Crag 70-odd years ago we were always entranced by the peregrines, with swept-back wings, which dived out of the sky like fighter aircraft – the most exciting birds in Lakeland, we thought. Then, for years, we rarely saw them and, after the war, heard that pesticides (notably DDT – later banned from use) had vastly reduced their numbers. But now we hear the peregrine is back in the fells in greater numbers than ever before, and I know of many nesting sites. A peregrine used to live in a limestone quarry adjoining the golf course at the back of my house but disappeared when nearby land was used for waste disposal. Now he's back again on another quarry cliff just round the corner.

Just after the war a climbing friend, Tom Philipson of Kendal, who was a devoted ornithologist, lowered me on a rope to a peregrine's nest on Buckbarrow, the big climbing crag in Longsleddale. I had to mark the egg with indelible ink so that it would be unsaleable to collectors who regularly robbed nests of valuable eggs. I remember putting my initials, AHG, on the egg and Tom then hauled me back up the crag. In the summer of 1949, I managed to lead a new severe-level climb on the crag I called Sadgill Wall, which went past the nesting site. Tom was with me and my second was a very old friend, Eric Arnison of Penrith. The reason I was leading such distinguished company was that we had all failed to get up our intended first pitch in clinker-nailed boots until I found some old plimsolls in my rucksack, which made things easier, and the other two managed, with great skill, to follow in their nails. Wonderful youthful days when the crags were our playground.

CHAPTER FIVE

Water, Water Everywhere

ONE OF THE ambitions of *Guardian* contributors in the 1950s was to 'write a Miscellany', to persuade the deputy editor, Paddy Monkhouse, to take 1500 words for the paper's most popular features slot. The standards of the Miscellany column were high and a premium was placed on elegant writing as well as an interesting subject. This was as obvious a challenge for Harry Griffin as a chain of tiny holds across some perpendicular rockface with a climber's nickname such as Blasphemy Crack, and a classification of v. severe.

His first success came on 14 November 1959 with an account of two Grasmere men, an odd couple whose mission in life appealed to Monkhouse's enjoyment of whimsy, provided it was anchored in the real world rather than self-consciously eccentric. Timothy Tyson was 76 that year but still working as the village cobbler and an expert on mountain boots. Colin Dodgson was 49 and ran the tea gardens in Grasmere (only one in those distant days) where his

Kendal mint cake was specially renowned. Both loved the fells and decided to organise their passion by climbing every peak over 2000ft in the National Park.

A précis of their adventures formed a short feature by Harry but it was his second *Guardian* encounter with the pair which made it into Miscellany. Flushed with their peak-bagging triumph, Tyson and Dodgson decided to follow it by bathing in every mountain tarn in the Lakes. There are more than 400 of these, ranging from proper-sized lakes to very large puddles. The thing they have in common is very chilly water indeed.

'The end of the long, cold story came the other day, when shivering in a shower of hail, they scrambled out of a tarn high on a shoulder of Esk Pike and shook hands.' Thus wrote Harry on the end of the epic, which saw the two men bathe in 463 tarns, frequently having to break the ice to get in because Dodgson's tea garden business meant that most of their trips had to be done in the tourist off-season in winter. Once, in Martindale, they had to dig down through snow to find the tarn at all. They plotted the deepest (Blea Water in Mardale), largest (Devoke Water), smallest (Foxes Tarn) and highest (un-named, on Broad Crag at 2750ft) – although the last was to become a matter of great debate which gave much Diary material to Harry.

The other great role of tarns and becks for *Guardian* readers was as places where Harry and assorted companions went skinny-dipping. He couldn't pass one in the summer without stripping off, plunging in and then returning to the typewriter to explain how he managed to get away without other fellwalkers seeing. The Coniston Tigers always bathed nude beyond their hut on the promontory near Coniston Hall – 'something which you couldn't do today,' wrote Harry, adding mischievously, 'at least not with propriety'. On August Bank Holiday in 1964 his grumbles about the sheer number of 'weekend amateurs' on the fells were forgotten when he saw three of them skinny-dipping in Glenridding beck as

The Diarist at his desk. The typewriter was an Adler Gabriele 35 and the view stretched away to the fells above Kendal town hall clock
(courtesy of Sandra Parr)

boldly as any Tiger, each with a can of beer. In his sixties, on one of the last walks with his brother Leslie, he swam naked in a hailstorm in Easedale Tarn and then the pair of them walked back starkers to the edge of Grasmere before getting dressed in a copse. The weather was so foul that there was no one else around to see.

That occasion, and many others, owed something to a German doctor who was one of the intellectuals Harry got to know at the Wastwater Hotel as a teenager. This man proselytised for the benefits of not drying after a mountain dip, on the grounds that the water would go back into the body and restore its energy. Harry experimented in Lingmell beck at Down-in-the-Dale, not far from the hotel. He was never convinced by the notion of water re-entering the pores but he said that somehow his clothes remained dry, so he followed the German's method for the rest of his life. He also robustly ignored his schoolteacher who had warned about mountain stream water and upset stomachs. 'What are becks for if not for drinking?' Harry wrote.

His research was also prompted by plans for a book called *Music and Mountains*, which he left almost finished on his death. One chapter is wholly devoted to tarns under the heading 'Eyes of the Mountain', which he borrowed from his friend the painter W. Heaton Cooper (another initial man), whose evocative tan and russet water-colours Harry much admired. Latterly, he spent a lot of time at one particular tarn, Lanty's, a particularly intriguing and very beautiful one, lying serenely on the slopes of Helvellyn but almost certainly named after a smuggler and hooch distiller called Lanty Slee. All these ingredients were grist to the Country Diary but they had a personal importance as well. Lanty's was the favourite tarn of Harry's last companion, Josie Clegg, and her ashes are scattered there.

There will almost certainly be a Griffin Tarn one day, chosen from one of a surprisingly large number which have somehow evaded a name. But enthusiasts jumped the gun on this one, prompting a growl from the Coniston Tiger in one of his last Country Diaries. The 'large but rather dreary' pool to which he refers would make a very good target for a day's walk, especially as you can hike on the way across Helm Crag, one of the loveliest and most exciting of the Lake District's smaller fells. From there, the path follows the ridge via Gibson Knott and Rough Crag to the lower slopes of Steel Fell, and there you can make up your mind whether Harry's protestations were genuine or a front, and should be respected or ignored. Another ridge to Easedale or a boggy trek down Greenburn Bottom takes you back to Grasmere, where every other building in the village now offers the equivalent of Colin Dodgson's tea garden in the 1950s.

Underwater world
⚡ August 1955 ⚡

There must have been more bathing in the lakes, tarns and pools this summer than for many a long year. Warm bathing too – the sort where you can stay in for hours. My last swim was in the loop of a lazy beck which for most of its winding miles has been not much more than a trickle among the boulders in recent weeks. But at one point, close to some grazing fell ponies, there was a tempting 30 yards' stretch where the shingle dropped suddenly into a long, still pool. A shoal of minnows vanished in a flash and a nice brown trout streaked through the shallows as we slithered in. An earlier bathe had been in quite a different Westmorland river – 20ft deep a yard from its canyon-like sides but so narrow that even a poor swimmer could feel safe. We were trying out some amateur frogman equipment and I was seeing the underwater world for the first time. Once under the surface, we seemed to be in a vast, silent Aladdin's cave, strangely illuminated by an eerie light. The stillness and the quiet were almost ghostly. What little movement we saw – among the weeds for instance – seemed slow and sleepy. A huge salmon – half spent, we thought – lay motionless in the shade of a rock. We could have got him, had we felt that way, with a pronged spear. A score or more trout zig-zagged across the pool quite leisurely as if we were part of the scenery. A few feet away two or three eels wriggled lazily, like the dark shadows of waving leaves. It was disappointing not to be able to stay down in that strange, fairy world a little longer.

The marathon swimmers
JULY 1957

Yet another enthusiast plans to set off this weekend to swim the ten-and-a-half miles' length of Windermere. Last Sunday three of them completed the distance, making a total of 40 successes since a Mr Foster of Oldham first performed the feat in 1911. In the intervening half-century the lake has twice been swum there and back (21 miles) and has also been conquered by school-children, a middle-aged married woman, 15-year-old twins and in the dark. It has been swum by a naval commander, a baths superintendent, a jeweller, a lorry driver, a mineral water manufacturer, a fireman and a moulder. Six years ago a major in the Greek Army swam it four times (in the year) and recently a young girl did most of it on her back. And in September up to a score of people will be attempting the feat – racing against one another. Whether any of these determined people really enjoy their slow struggles is questionable. It is the lesser fry like myself who manage to enjoy their Lake swimming, or perhaps we should call it merely bathing. At the end of one of the many recent scorching days on the fells the zenith of luxury has been an exhilarating plunge from close-cropped turf into a deep, dark pool, overhung with rowans and dappled with evening sunlight.

The climbers' springs
JUNE 1958

Every climber knows the little spring bubbling out of the rock at the foot of Dow Crag, near Coniston. Winter and summer it is always there and nature has even provided a little cup-shaped trough from which to drink. But there are dozens more of these little founts of clear, cold water which never dry up in the worst drought – one near the foot of Great Gully on Pavey Ark, another near Kern Knotts on Great Gable, a third just below the summit of Crinkle Crags and many more, if you know where to look. One of them is even marked on the one-inch Ordnance Survey map – Brownrigg Well, only three minutes' walk from the summit of Helvellyn. Hundreds of thirsty walkers pass this way in summer without realizing that sparkling refreshment is available only a short distance below the track across the stony top. It is even possible to drink from an unexpected supply among the Great Gable summit boulders – a trough of rainwater on a flat-topped rock which seems able to withstand the hottest sunshine. Red Tarn is sometimes described as the Lake District's highest tarn but there are in fact small ones rather higher – one or two of them on actual summits. Red Screes, for instance, has a tarn – sometimes containing perhaps the highest living tadpoles in England – within a few yards of its summit, and so does the rather lower Thunacar Knott in the Langdales. But the springs have the better water.

Waterfall staircase
✺ AUGUST 1958 ✺

One of the few things worth doing in the Lake District on a really wet day – a clarty day, we would call it – is looking at waterfalls. An even better thing, if you are of the adventurous type or just plain stupid, depending on how you view these things, is to climb one. The argument is that having decided to go out on the fells and get wet (without seeing any scenery), one might as well do the job properly just for the fun of it, and have a bit of excitement thrown in. Some routes up Lake District crags are delightfully described in the books as 'an ideal wet weather climb'; the one we tackled the other day was summed up by 'the greater the volume of water, the greater the difficulty and interest'. The one merit of this particular route was that one became drenched through to the skin immediately after starting, thus avoiding the unpleasant ordeal of getting wet through by degrees. Being really wet through is no discomfort, they say, provided one keeps moving. The climbing difficulties proved to be slight, but communications were trying. Because of the thunder and the crash of the pounding water it was impossible to hear oneself speak, let alone the other, and when out of sight of each other with the rope churning in the torrent we savoured, through the spray, the 'interest' mentioned in the guidebook.

British weather
❧ JANUARY 1960 ❧

What a fantastic transformation of the countryside within the space of a day! Yesterday morning we awoke to a white world, the snow inches deep on the lawns and feet deep in drifts on the passes, while today we are suddenly in the midst of the worst floods for a long time. The river, one of the fastest-flowing in England, they say, is racing through our little town this afternoon in a relentless brown torrent, bearing with it great trees, henhouse roofs and oil drums, besides many, many millions of tons of melted snow from the fells. People in the riverside houses, anxiously watching the rising waters all day, are now bringing up their valuables out of the cellars and taking up the carpets in the lower rooms. Some of them remember the last time, when the kitchen table floated underneath the ceiling. A little way out of the town, the roads are flooded right across in places, and acres of fields are under water. Trees, fences and telegraph poles are growing out of the water, and the sheep and cattle are huddled together, rather sorrowful-looking, on tiny islands. This evening the angry river, churning and boiling in its brown fury, swirled across the roadway into the first cellars. It will be an anxious night for many. What will the morning bring?

The diatomite tarn
JULY 1962

An edict from Whitehall directs that a local man may not dig up the diatomaceous earth from around one of our lonely tarns, and so these lovely jewels of the mountains slide into the news. Only a week or so ago they had divers scouring the bed of one of our best known tarns for the assorted junk thrown in over the years by residents and visitors. Altogether there are something like 460 tarns in the Lake District – the biggest the size of a small lake and the smallest little more than a pool caught high up among the crags. The diatomaceous earth, or diatomite, formed from the crustaceous remains of minute animal life and useful nowadays for a hundred commercial needs, may be found around this little-visited tarn which squats on a shelf a thousand feet up among heather-covered fells. Down in the valley a few miles away they dig it out in great buckets and the only other similar industry is in the distant Isle of Skye. But our little tarn is to be left for the birds – the black-headed gull, the sheld duck, the little grebe and the great whooper swans which flap noisily in every October and stay until May. Few people pass this way apart from the occasional bird-watcher or fisherman, so that the tarn can be the ideal place for a restful summer's evening. People are unlikely to get rid of their unwanted bicycles, prams and motorcar tyres within its reedy depths as they apparently do in the other, more popular, tarns. But then, there's no metalled highway to our little tarn, and no farm-house teas for the tourist when he gets there.

Crossing the bay
◆ SEPTEMBER 1989 ◆

Far out on the sands at low tide, with distant shores a vague blur on the horizon and the hills hidden in mist, it seemed a long way from anywhere and even lonely – although there were 200 in the party. Certainly, without Cedric Robinson, the Queen's Guide to the Sands, we should have been lost and compasses unavailing. For not only was there no distant aiming point but we took a curious curving course – halfway to Morecambe, it seemed – and then swung back, perhaps eight miles in all. We did it to cross the river channels at no more than knee depth to avoid the shifting quicksands that, over the centuries, have claimed many lives. It was the way to the Lakes long before the coming of the railways, and from at least the time of Henry VIII. Coaches ran daily over the sands at one time, as well as private carriages – the Duke of Edinburgh has driven a team across – and herds or flocks of cattle and sheep were guided or swam through the channels. The day before our crossing the guide had surveyed the route, as the channels are constantly changing, and marked out the safe places with laurel branches, seen in the distance as black specks. He halted us before each crossing for instructions – 'Spread out between the markers and keep behind me' – and then we waded into the current; grannies and children among us with dogs happily paddling across. Vast flocks of birds were feeding in the far shallows, and scurrying shapes towards the horizon were picked out through binoculars as the tractors of the fluke fishermen. Most crossed in bare feet or in trainers. I wore old mountain boots that took a week to dry out, and collected toe blisters from the chafing salt and sand.

Tumbling waters
‿ DECEMBER 1991 ‿

Many years ago, before they deepened the channel of the River Kent
flowing through the middle of Kendal, I watched a pair of swans
sailing majestically down flooded Stramongate, one of the main
streets in the town. We don't get floods like that now but the Kent,
one of the fastest flowing rivers in England, has been extremely high
recently, surging and swirling just under the town's bridges and
turning my thoughts to waterfalls. This is the time, after drenching
days of winter rain, sleet or snow, for looking at waterfalls. Lodore,
not the biggest nor the best of our falls, but, with Aira Force, among
the most popular, was recently looking exactly as the Poet Laureate
described it 170 years ago, but my preference is for more out-of-
the-way, if smaller, cataracts. Whorneyside Force at the foot of Hell
Gill in Oxendale was in splendid spate the other day, with tons of
water crashing angrily down the rocks. The fall makes a moderate
scramble in a dry summer and an attractive ice climb when frozen
into a white curtain in winter, but you couldn't get near it the other
day, nor even hear yourself speak. These Oxendale waterfalls – the
fine trinity of Bronney Gill, Crinkle Gill and Hell Gill – sometimes
provide foaming cascades of 150ft and more while the upper falls of
Dungeon Gill are far more impressive than the 'tourist' fall, over
which Ruskin enthused. The longest single fall in the district is
probably Scale Force near Crummock Water, sufficiently remote to
have been more a favourite with Victorian tourists than the motor
car trippers of today – but Cam Spout on Scafell crashing down
the crags like an avalanche in our wildest dale head is a far finer
spectacle than the picture-postcard cascade. The district is still alive
with the sight and sound of hundreds of new runners, becks and
gills – millions of tons of water careering out of control down the
fellsides and dazzling in their abandon.

Lanty's Tarn

ᘓᕼ JANUARY 1994 ᘓᕼ

A stroll up the frozen fellside from Glenridding to Lanty's Tarn and a return down Grisedale nicely filled in a sunny January morning, sparkling with frost and distant snows. A few years ago, walking down the superbly scenic north-east ridge of St Sunday Crag, I had pointed out to my companion the lovely, little tarn nestling among Scots pines just across the trough of Grisedale. The sun was shining through the trees on to the tarn burnishing it like a jewel or a pool in a fairy tale. She was entranced by both the picture and the name and immediately decided to call her new flat 'Lanty's'. This recent trip was to take a colour photograph of the tarn for her drawing room. Who Lanty was – it is a fairly common Lakeland diminutive for Lancelot – I've no idea but the tarn is clearly artificial – perhaps dammed, probably by the Marshall family, last century. There is a tiny ruined building nearby and this is said to have been the store for ice collected from the tarn and kept insulated in sawdust until the summer months when it was probably used by the big house, Patterdale Hall. Perhaps the tarn was created for this purpose. Its situation, perched high above Glenridding Beck and Grisedale, is superb and the pines complete the picture. A short stroll away is the summit of Keldas – one of the most delightful 1000ft summits in the district and a splendid viewpoint for Ullswater, framed between the Scots pines. Just below the tarn and the summit is the tiny community of Grassthwaitehow where are kennelled the hounds of the Ullswater pack; no matter how quietly you creep down the fellside they will hear you and start up their yelping. A day or two later I celebrated my 83rd birthday by a walk from Ambleside up Wansfell Pike which, because of its tourist popularity, I have probably ascended fewer times than any other Lakeland fell. Indeed, on a very warm evening about 20 years ago, two of us failed to get up, collapsing halfway up, because of the excessive humidity, and having to be revived later in the Golden Rule. This time, however, the ascent was very worthwhile because of the magnificent view of the snowbound western skyline from the Coniston fells to Red Screes with a tiny sliver of Scafell just visible beyond the Three Tarns gap and the topmost inches of Seafell Pike rising high above Bowfell Buttress. Without the sunlit snow it would have been difficult to spot higher land beyond Crinkles ridge.

Buttermere days
∽ MARCH 1998 ∾

Not a cloud in the sky, the sunny slopes of Mellbreak perfectly mirrored in the surface of Crummock Water and a few Herdwicks wandering along the unfenced lakeshore road. This was a recent, still morning in lovely Buttermere – in many respects, my favourite Lakeland valley – where, once again, we had been staying for a short holiday.

One day, on our way up Robinson, by way of Buttermere Moss, I recalled a previous, rather more challenging, visit 60 years ago when, from our car on Honister Pass, we had already traversed Fleetwith Pike, Haystacks, High Crag, High Stile and Red Pike. We had also consumed, in the Fish Hotel, several pints of foaming beer, served, I remember sadly, in those most suitable, but now rarely seen, receptacles – glazed earthenware tankards. As a result, our traverse (of Robinson, Hindscarth and Dale Head) that followed was rather trying, but quickly forgotten during the consumption of a vast mutton pie in Mrs Edmondson's kitchen at Seathwaite. The mutton, as always, had been slowly cooked all day in her fireplace oven, and, as they say, 'just fell away'. Even now, I smack my lips, in memory.

But, the other day, we were merely pottering up Robinson, enjoying the fantastic view from the comparatively lowly summit of

High Snockrigg (1725ft). Buttermere and Crummock Water, with the smoke from the farms and cottages drifting across the meadows, seemed directly below our boots and the steep, wooded fells across the dale, split by the hanging necklace of Sour Milk Gill, looked a vertical mountain wall. The best views are by no means always from the highest places.

The hidden waterfalls

～ SEPTEMBER 1998 ～

If you're ever in the John Peel country at the 'back o' Skiddaw', it would be a pity not to explore the Howk at Caldbeck, for there's nothing quite like it anywhere else in the national park. The Howk – strangely among hills of volcanic rock – is a limestone ravine with natural caves and caverns beside thundering waterfalls, rushing torrents and inviting pools, not unlike certain exciting corners in the Yorkshire Dales. Indeed, a first view of the place may remind you of Gordale Scar.

You enter the ravine by walking along a track, shadowed by trees, from the crowded duck pond on the village green, and after a little way, step out into an open area of towering crags, and the sight and sound of falling water. Surprisingly, you see the massive ruins of a considerable building of enormous, red sandstone blocks, but the shape and situation of the remains, and nearly 150 years of weathering, almost makes them fit into the landscape. This was the famous bobbin mill once said to have had the largest waterwheel in the country. Nowadays, you pass through the gorge along a fenced way with many stone steps, and further on a wooden bridge across the beck, and carry on, if you like, to the main road.

Many years ago, with a mountaineering friend, we did some scrambling around the rocks and caverns but this doesn't seem to be encouraged nowadays. And, much longer ago, the Victorians came from far and wide to view the waterwheel and to picnic in and around the caves. To fill in your day, you can have a look at John Peel's ornate gravestone, or that of the 'Beauty of Buttermere', in the crowded churchyard, or, better still, walk up High Pike, the most northerly two-thousander in Lakeland.

Eau naturel

∽ AUGUST 1999 ✑

From the High Street ridge, on a recent warm, windy day, we dropped down the contours to Hayeswater and the stony track to Hartsop. It was on these slopes, about 70 years ago, that I saw my first red deer and fell ponies – the deer, briefly outlined on the ridge just ahead of us before plunging down to Riggindale, and the fell ponies, half a dozen of them, quietly grazing the slopes above the reservoir.

I remember the docility of the wild-looking ponies as we stroked them, their unkempt manes blowing in the breeze and their long shaggy tails almost sweeping the ground. But no deer or fell ponies to be seen the other day – just the western hills of Lakeland spread along the horizon with the pointed peak of Catstycam, one of the shapeliest of our mountains, prominent in the middle. Hayeswater, Penrith's water supply, was almost brimming the spill-way and Hayeswater Gill, a sparkling necklace of pools, waterfalls and cascades, danced down the fellside in merry spate. How often, in past years, have I bathed in these pools on exhaustingly hot days?

The finest pools, all overhung with mountain ash, are above the filter house but these are a little too public for those bathing without a costume, which was always my state. My own favourite place, therefore, for a dip at the end of a walk was usually a tiny, secluded pool, shaded by rowans, with a waterfall at one end, just before Hartsop and close to the gill's junction with Pasture Beck.

It's only a few yards from the track but beautifully concealed: nobody has ever spotted me there, cooling off au naturel. I had another look at the pool the other day – just the same as I remembered, cool and, even now, almost inviting. And I can easily recall dozens of other 'secret' places for the nude bathing in the fells, hard by tracks and other places. Perhaps the cheekiest is a pool in the Derwent, close to Seathwaite farm on the way to Stokeley Bridge, where I have bathed more than once, just below the track, unseen by walkers passing above. But now, sadly, these lovely places no longer have the same appeal.

On ice

❧ DECEMBER 2002 ❧

There was a tiny sprinkling of snow – rather like grains of salt – on my bathroom window one morning recently and, a few miles to the north-east, a fine, white dusting on the Whinfell ridge and along the tops of the Howgills. It was a raw, misty morning with a biting east wind but I thought I could also spot a hint of proper snow on the distant high fells almost hidden in cloud. For me, this was the first snow of the winter – always an exciting moment for any skier or mountaineer anxious to be off to the hills.

For several reasons, I have not been in the fells for some time and outings in the last two years have been confined to small hills, but at 92 years of age (in a week or two) I can still enthuse about them. And, for almost as long as I can remember, snowbound hills, especially when sunlit, have had a very special appeal. There has always seemed, to me, so many things you can do in winter when there's snow on the fells with the hills and crags looking twice as big and far more spectacular and exciting. Besides snow and ice climbing in the gullies or on the crags there's walking the tops in the snow, downhill skiing, ski touring, ski mountaineering and ice skating, although it's some years since I used to skate, every winter, on Rydal Water and Tarn Hows. And once, in 1929, I skated from Lakeside to the Ferry and back on Windermere, frozen all over with ice thick enough to hold dozens of cars and hundreds of people. One wonders, with this early December snow, which quickly disappeared, whether we might get a good outdoors winter this time – something, with global warming, we have been denied for many years.

Eyes of the mountain
NOVEMBER 2003

'Eyes of the mountain.' This is how my old friend, William Heaton Cooper, the painter, described tarns – pools high in the hills that reflected the sky and brought it down just in front of you or, perhaps, into the middle distance. Heaton was always painting tarns, sitting at his easel in remote fells, and there are scores of his paintings and drawings of them in his definitive work on the tarns of Lakeland. And, at the recent Grasmere exhibition to mark the centenary of his birth – he died several years ago – there were other paintings of tarns not seen by the general public before.

I had known Heaton for more than half a century and owe him a great deal for it was he, and Alfred Wainwright, who encouraged me to write my first book 43 years ago. Heaton's favourite tarn, 'the most completely satisfying of all the tarns of Lakeland', was Sprinkling Tarn, under the crags of Great End and near the track to Esk Hause, the very hub of mountain Lakeland. It was 'the character and feel of the place' that most attracted him. I could name at least a dozen favourite tarns but find difficulty in deciding the very best. The dozen would certainly include Josie's resting place, Lanty Tarn, and three tarns in the Coniston fells where I first rock-climbed 75 years ago – Goatswater, Low Water and Blind

Tarn. But there are also Hard Tarn, high-up below the Helvellyn ridge, where I once had my coldest-ever bathe, Lambfoot Dub above the Corridor Route to Scafell Pike and many, many others. But I hesitantly question Heaton's 'highest tarn' – Broadcrag Tarn. Long Top Tarn on Crinkle Crags is higher – but it probably all depends on how exactly you define a tarn.

What's in a name?
❧ MAY 2004 ❧

As gracefully as I could manage it I have declined the possible distinction of an eponymous tarn. Anxious to mark the alleged contribution to the district of my books and other writings, a correspondent has been zealously canvassing authorities and individuals for an unnamed tarn at the head of Greenburn near Grasmere to be called Griffin Tarn. I am dead against this – and not just because the pool is pretty undistinguished. If pressed I could give a dozen reasons for my intransigence, one being that this is a very old joke. Many years ago two of my mountain friends used to call this large but rather dreary pool Griffin's Tarn because I was 'always going on about it'.

Although the tarn is about 300ft long it was not marked on any map until the late 1980s. Several years before then I had felt so strongly about this that I wrote to the Ordnance Survey suggesting they should, at least, show the tarn on the map even if they didn't give it a name and, sure enough, they later drew in its distinctive blue shape. I don't necessarily claim to have put the tarn on the map for Heaton Cooper, in his earlier definitive book on Lakeland tarns, had described and drawn the tarn, calling it Steel Fell Tarn. My suggested name, to the Ordnance Survey, had been Boundary Tarn since it lies on the former boundary between Cumberland and Westmorland but they took no notice of this. And they haven't shown this county boundary for many years. There are dozens of unnamed tarns in Lakeland but this one is possibly the largest of them. Thirty years ago Griffin's Tarn was a joke between three old friends. I thank my correspondent for his zeal but this should remain a joke.

CHAPTER SIX

Sunshine and Snow

DESCRIPTIONS of the beautiful landscape of the Lake District are notoriously prone to cliché; mountains loom, snow sparkles and the lights of the inn twinkle cheerfully at the end of the path from the fells. Sometimes the obvious words are the best ones and Harry uses his share of them. But his Diaries are suffused by two characteristics which are particular trademarks of his writing.

He often comments on how still the mountains are and how nothing is moving apart from the occasional falling leaf or a sheep browsing slowly from one grassy slope to another. But there was always one other thing on the go and that was Harry himself. He might spend periods sitting wreathed in pipesmoke or waving it aside to contemplate the view, but he was mostly on the move. The sense of a man who has picked up the scent, and got his eyes and ears wide open, brings his descriptions of the landscape alive.

He was also much higher than all the *Guardian*'s other Country

Diarists, literally so. Enid Wilson nosed about the Lake District valleys, he used to say, while he marched along the summit ridges. This gave him experiences and views which bewitch us because few of us have shared them. He can raise goosebumps with his description from a sunlit peak of virtually the whole of Lakeland blanketed in cotton-wool mist beneath his feet; only the pyramid tops of other high summits poking up above the cloud like triangular islands.

Many of the diaries draw on both this high-altitude tableland and Harry's multifarious activities once he had got up there. For many years, for example, he received a framed certificate from the Royal Society for the Protection of Cruelty to Animals for his voluntary work as a skilled climber, rescuing cragfast – or stuck – sheep. The bird protectors likewise used him to mark eggs in the nests of threatened peregrine falcon families. It is typical of Harry the journalist, however, that he was able not only to describe the wonders of the hawks, whose side he and the *Guardian*'s readers would naturally take, but also to hint at the appeal to the curious and lively mind of egg-collecting, and the not entirely unsympathetic character of some of the enthusiasts for what has now become a crime.

That element of detachment found in the best reporters was useful for him in dealing with such issues; meanwhile the short, if enthusiastic, attention span of most journalists helped with another of his best subjects, the weather. If Britain is famous for constantly changing weather, that is writ large in mountain country. Sun, rain, hail and snow whirl across the few hundred square miles of the Lake District in constant succession. From one of his high perches, Harry delighted in being able to see up to a dozen different varieties of weather affecting the area between the Pennines and the Irish Sea, all at the same time. He describes a rainstorm approaching and calculates how long it will take to arrive. He carried with him a chart which gave the maximum distance an object should be visible in relation to the observer's height above sea level. He never shrank from using meteorological language; 'anti-cyclonic gloom' was a favourite. He was awestruck by encounters with the Brocken Spectre, a ghostly effect when low sun magnifies a climber's shadow onto mist below, named after the highest peak in Germany's Harz mountains where it was first recorded. And with a minimum of adjectives or overblown colour, he evokes immediately the clear light of low winter suns or the haze of summer over Lakeland for those who have enjoyed them in the past but are now far away. He drew too on a rich memory of events such as the 1929 Great Freeze, when he skated round braziers and parked cars on Windermere whose ice was a foot thick.

Harry also zipped about on skis, his favourite method of travel apart from his two long, rangy legs. Typically, he got involved in promoting a sport from which he took so much pleasure himself. Although his first wife Mollie retired early from the field after breaking a leg at ski school in Austria when they had not long been married, Harry brought on scores of young skiers on Raise, the fell best suited to organized downhill skiing in the Lakes. He was a founder-member in 1936 of the Lake District ski club and one of a sturdy group who manhandled bits of an old tractor engine, hundreds of yards of rope and an entire hut 2500ft up the mountain, to organize the first crude version of an Alpine chalet café and ski-tow. They had to carry the hut up twice. Soon after its first installation, a gale blew it back down the mountain.

This hard graft gave Harry a particularly powerful feeling for snow and a great ability to describe its many faces, moods and varieties. Although his longest and most dramatic runs were in the Alps and the immaculately groomed runs of western Canada (he marvelled like a boy at their sophistication and modern technology), he had plenty of memorable British ski adventures to recount. One Midsummer's Day it was possible to ski on Cross Fell, the peak of the Pennine chain, where Harry at other times recorded wind speeds of 108 and even 134mph. Just once, he was able to ski all the way from a summit to a pub – the top of the Helvellyn and Dodds ridge to the Royal Inn at Dockray – as people commonly do in the Alps.

The sun brought him out too, often in later years with his celebrated 'Compo' bobble hat, named after the eccentric Yorkshireman in the long-running Northern TV comedy, *Last of the Summer Wine*. Until one of the Pennine gales blew it away, as he describes regretfully in one of these 'weather Diaries', this protected his increasingly bald head on very hot days (and for all the Lake District's deservedly rainy reputation, he suffered from sunburn on several occasions as a young climber). From beneath the woolly hat, his fluffy white hair flew out like the wings on Mercury's helmet.

Harry covered the Great Drought of 1976 but his most impressive descriptions followed walks or climbs in tempestuous weather. He was able to keep going in truly foul conditions, without the curious extra protection of another writer and photographer, Walter Poucher, whose mountain panoramas he much admired. Poucher was a manager in Yardley's perfume company and he used his own products, including lipstick and foundation cream, for extra warmth during long, cold waits on the fells until the light was at its best for his photographs. Harry's only recorded connection between cosmetics and the mountains was on his first long-distance hike in the Alps when he left the group's only bar of soap outside the tent on the first night. 'I never made that mistake again,' he said. 'It was eaten by goats and we were a very smelly party when we got to the end of our trek.'

Weather wisdom

SEPTEMBER 1962

One of the most useless pieces of weather information to have by you so far as the Lake District is concerned is the couplet which begins: 'Red sky at night is the shepherd's delight.' As often as not the exact reverse is the truth and this applies equally to the rest of the adage. There have been two good examples of the unreliability of this old saw within the last ten days – an incredibly shocking day following a magnificent golden sunset, and a bright sunny day – one of the few this summer, unexpectedly chasing an unusually vivid morning. All that one can do is to distrust a red sky most heartily whether it occurs in the evening or the morning, so that occasionally you might get a pleasant surprise. 'Too bright, too early' is often a fairly reasonable guide, while an exceptional sunset nearly always precedes a remarkable day. The unfortunate thing is that the day is just as likely to be remarkable for rain as for sunshine. Farmers are popularly supposed to be infallible weather prophets but they must never be relied upon outside their own few acres. To them a patch of mist or cloud on a distant top or the wind coming from behind a particular wood might be of great significance but take them into the next parish and they're lost. They might sniff the air, or throw straws into the wind, or even – though I've never seen them do it – put up a moistened finger but they've really no more idea than you or me. And you've only got to listen to the BBC forecasts to realise that the mountains make their own weather.

Skiing in the sun
❧ DECEMBER 1962 ❧

On a day this week when most of England seemed lost in fog I drove up an old road into the Westmorland hills through the sparkling sunshine of a perfect winter afternoon. It was a day for superlatives as most of the days have been this week in the fell country. The sky was cloudless and blue, the air crisp and clear with views right across the Lake District, and the day so calm that the woodsmoke from the cottage chimneys rose straight as the Borrowdale birches. In the meadows by the river the cattle stood transfixed like wooden models, bemused perhaps by the stillness and sunlight, and at the foot of the hill road two men in shirt sleeves were laying a hedge and whistling as they worked. A farmer with two dogs at heel and a gun over his shoulder came striding down the frozen fellside and two girls in jodhpurs astride sleek brown ponies came trotting out of a side lane. Near the top of the fell I found what I had come for – a long patch of hard snow, tilted at the right angle and full of sunshine. My stolen hour of skiing was watched only by my dog and, too soon, it was time to go. For ten minutes I watched a blazing sun dip down through an orange sky towards the western hills – the perfect ending to a lovely winter's day. Already night had come down into the valley, but in the hills it was still afternoon. Two silent jet aircraft, golden specks in the late sunlight, made golden trails across the purpling sky and the sun rimmed the outline of the distant hills in gold. I drove down across the crackling pools and the frost-caked road towards the valley and the evening lamplight, while a crescent moon shone clear out of a darkening sky.

Getting very wet
༅ AUGUST 1963 ༆

When you've been wet through to the skin on the fells more often than you can remember, there comes a time, if past your first youth, when you resolve never again to set off on a hill expedition on a really clarty day. Of course, if you're caught in the downpour later it's a different matter. I made my resolve some years ago but seem to break it regularly, the last time being only the other day when two of us set out for some gentle mountain exercise and were well-soaked after only a quarter of an hour. But once you're wet through there's no particular point in turning back for you can't get any wetter and the exercise should keep you warm. It's the process of becoming wet through that's so trying – first the legs and thighs, then the arms and shoulders, and finally, miserably, the back. After that, there's a certain animal satisfaction in splashing through swollen becks or even crashing nonchalantly through tall, dripping brackens. Not to mention the inner reward for pressing on regardless. We couldn't get very far the other day, except for a brief moment during a snatched sandwich break on the 2500ft contour when the mists slowly parted to reveal a distant stretch of lake and then closed in again for good. Obviously, we thought, there'll be nobody out on the tops today but on the first summit a patch of yellow turned out to be half a dozen cheery Outward Bound boys in capes, while around another cairn a mile further on there was another cluster of them, poring over dog-eared maps and fiddling with compasses. 'Helvellyn's this way,' said one of them to us, more for reassurance than as a piece of information. We agreed, set them happily on their way, and turned down steep runnels of scree into the combe.

Days of haze

SEPTEMBER 1966

For days now the hills have been hidden – not by mist and cloud but by the sleepy haze of late summer. Overhead, the cloudless blue zenith scratched here and there by the white vapour trails of unseen aircraft, but in the shadowy distance the lower fells merge into the haze or hang, as faint grey smudges, above the trees. There is no real horizon, for the edge of the world may be only a couple of fields away and the air is so still that falling leaves may be watched, singly, as they float leisurely down to earth. The lakes, overhung with white morning mists, are as smooth as burnished silver and the tarns sparkle like jewels in the afternoon sunlight. Already the leaves are beginning to turn but the full glory of the red, gold and bronze of autumn has yet to come. The farmers have trimmed their hedges and in a field below my windows the yellow corn is stacked, throwing long shadows across the stubble. The holidaymakers are still about. More discerning visitors, say the shopkeepers and the hoteliers, here to enjoy the scenery at leisure and not just trippers up for the run and out for a good time among the crowds. So that family parties and teenagers have given place to quieter folk in tweeds, with walking sticks and cameras. There may be morning fog in the little towns that encircle the sanctuary, but you soon climb into the hazy sunshine and a warmth we could have done with weeks ago. But carry on up into the fells and in an hour or so you will be able to step on to high ridges with views from Yorkshire to Scotland and, below your feet, a half-hidden Lake District preparing for its winter sleep.

A splendidly appalling day
◈ OCTOBER 1969 ◈

Eight days ago we had one of the most splendidly appalling mountain days I can ever remember in the Lake District – neatly sandwiched between two days of sunny, autumn glory. Ordinary rain and wind can almost be expected in the hills and heavy rain and strong winds are common enough but the conditions this Sunday went far beyond the usual limits. The rain, for instance, came down at times in something like the volume you might expect to encounter below a bursting dam and you could see it afar off – huge, grey curtains of water sweeping down upon you. This could have been borne with equanimity after the first few minutes – for once you are soaked to the skin and can't get any wetter it's all rather pleasant – had it not been for the wind. I've often been blown over by the wind on the fells but I can't remember its happening four or five times in one afternoon before, and there was one occasion when I must have been airborne for several feet and found the rocky landing quite tricky. There were, in fact, nearly 20 of us being blown all over the mountain and our problems were hardly lightened by our being engaged in the slightly incongruous task of carrying a quarter of a mile of rope, nearly two inches in diameter, up the mountain. This is to be our new ski tow and we will remember our battle through the maelstrom when the same, maddening rope is carrying us up the mountainside over the winter snows. To the outsider – had there been one about on such a day – we must have presented an extraordinary sight, but at least the hard work kept us warm – unlike the mountain ponies, corralled by the dam, their backs to the storm and looking miserable.

The mountain spectre
ᘓᘓ FEBRUARY 1971 ᘓᘓ

In nearly half a century of wanderings in the hills I have seen only four Brocken Spectres and the last one, encountered quite recently on the upper slopes of Bowfell, was unquestionably the best. Down in the valley, after a long succession of miserable, misty days, it had been a perfect February morning – warm sunshine, blue skies, not a breath of wind, and the tops festooned in white, diaphanous clouds that barely concealed tantalizing patches of sunlit snow. An hour later I was in the clouds, on the east ridge of the mountain, not far below the summit, admiring the play of the sunlight through the white, fleecy draperies when I sensed a movement or shadow to my right and, looking round, saw the Spectre, a hundred, two hundred feet high, astride a ridge across the bowl of Mickleden. I moved an arm, the vision did the same; I took a pace upwards and he strode in step across the skyline. The sun was directly behind me, coming over the top of Crinkle Crags through the broken cloud and my image, magnified many times, was photographed on the thin mists hanging high above the head of the dale. Framing the gigantic apparition in concentric circles were rainbows – three or four of them – in blue, gold, and red, and the whole vision moved up the mountain with me for a few yards and then vanished as quickly as it had come. From the summit the view was remarkable, snow patches disappearing below my feet into a vast sea of fleecy cloud above which floated the tops of the highest mountains. The Sca Fells were immediately recognized but I had to take a compass-bearing to confirm that one distant rocky island was the topmost crag of Glaramara.

Meeting a balloon
❧ DECEMBER 1972 ❧

Brocken Spectres, a one-legged motorcyclist on top of Coniston Old Man and a tourist with an umbrella on Scafell Pike, have been interesting but not especially unusual encounters in the hills. But my latest encounter – with a balloon – was something out of the ordinary. It was Christmas Eve – the best day there's been in the fells for weeks. The sun shone brightly all day long, the sky was cloudless all round the compass – apart from wisps of cottonwool over Thirlmere and a solid blanket of it over the Windermere valley – and there was new snow on the high fells. The previous night an iron frost had suddenly gripped the district and the 12ft wide cornices on Helvellyn were frozen rock-hard. It was when negotiating the last icy stretch on to Helvellyn Low Man that I saw the balloon – a blue sphere, glinting in the sunlight, just above the serrated saddle of Swirral Edge. At first I thought it some sort of meteorological balloon or perhaps a mountain rescue device secured to the rocks on the Edge but, having calculated that it must be at least half-a-mile away, I realized it was a manned balloon with men in it. It was hanging motionless above Red Tarn, just over 3000ft, with the High Street range for backcloth, and was a striking and colourful apparition to meet so high in the thin, cold air. As I watched, it slowly drifted northwards just clearing the snow-bound summit of Catstycam – on which three or four human specks could be seen – by less than 50ft, slid over the top of Raise and finally disappeared below the fells east of Stybarrow Dod – possibly into Deepdale. It seemed the ideal way to view the Lake District on such a perfect day.

Lord of the flies
ↀ SEPTEMBER 1991 ↀ

The hot, sultry weather has been far from ideal for tramping the fells since visibility, due to heat haze, has usually been very poor. On a recent traverse of Place Fell from Boardale Hause to Sandwick and back by the lake shore path – in clear weather, the fell a magnificent grandstand from which to view the eastern combes of Helvellyn – no fells at all could be seen and, from the top, even Ullswater no more than a shadowy blur. With no wind – the opposite of the weather forecast – flies were again an exasperating nuisance; perspiration, when stripped to the waist, clearly either attracts or annoys them. Only by the constant emission of pipe tobacco smoke – difficult when going steeply uphill – and the waving of towel or handkerchief could the irritation be marginally alleviated. But, inured as we are to the problem, we were hardly prepared for our reception at the summit – tens of thousands of insects in a vast, black swarm, perhaps 12ft across, seething above the cairn. I have often encountered these swarms around summit cairns but never so many as this plague that darkened the sky and had us scurrying away in a flash. I used to think these insect clouds around summit cairns might have been attracted by the decomposing remains of sandwiches stuffed away, unseen, among the stones but, nowadays, I'm more inclined to attribute them to the movement, or lack of it, of air although I can't understand it. Wind blows flies away but the summit of a fell is usually its windiest point and the last place, you think, they would chose for swarming; a sheltered hollow on a lee side would seem a more likely place but they always select a summit cairn. Still, I suppose they know what they're doing.

Losing the bobble hat
❧ NOVEMBER 1993 ❧

The first snow of the winter was encountered on a bitterly cold day when accompanying a friend collecting 'two-thousanders' in the High Street range. Warning of gale force winds on the tops, the local weather station advised winter clothing – a pretty obvious precaution with thick ice everywhere – although the ascent of Kidsty Pike from Mardale Head was straightforward with the south-east wind no more than a nuisance. But the short walk to the next summit, Rampsgill Head, across icy ground and new powder snow, proved, unexpectedly, something of an ordeal. With a moderate gale, Force 7 on the Beaufort Scale, there is difficulty in walking against the wind and 'whole trees are in motion' while with Force 8, a fresh gale, progress is impeded and twigs are broken off trees. Since there are no trees on these tops it was difficult to be precise about the exact number on the scale but we were certainly in some sort of a gale – although probably not a strong gale (Force 9) or a whole gale (Force 10) – for we were quite unable to move in one direction and, backs to the wind, found the utmost difficulty in avoiding being blown away. In the middle of it I suffered the sad loss of my woolly, bobbly hat, found on Helvellyn about 30 years ago and worn on hundreds of mountain trips since. We had just left the cairn on Rampsgill Head and were struggling north towards High Raise, trying to avoid being blown over the crags, when my head suddenly felt like a block of ice and, reaching up to my balding pate, I found I was bare-headed. A moment earlier I had been swathed in my woolly hat pulled down over my ears and kept in place by the hood of my anorak tied under my chin and, secondly, by the hood of my cagoule, similarly secured. But, despite all this tethering, the gale had torn everything apart and, for all I know, my precious 'Compo' hat may now be travelling down the water system from

Haweswater to Manchester. If you find it take care of it for me. After such a buffeting it was something of a contrast to sit in a sunny, sheltered corner below Kidsty Howes admiring the new snow gullies starting to appear beyond Riggindale; maybe, after a succession of disappointing winters for climbers and skiers, this may turn out to be a good snow season. No sign of golden eagles, fell ponies or red deer this time but Haweswater drawn down so low that the ruins of the old farms and lanes of Mardale Green, drowned 50 years ago, were plain to see.

Rainy day runners
SEPTEMBER 1994

All day long towering curtains of rain swept down Buttermere, dark, grey clouds crowded the summits and shattering gusts of wind whipped the waters of the lake, rattling the canvas of the marquee. A good day for snoozing over the fire with the Sunday papers but 150 people, in their twenties to their sixties, including a score of women, spent the day racing round the mountain tops, fighting their own private battles in the mist, rain, wind and piercing cold. It was the annual mountain trial, the country's most formidable test for fell runners, over a secret course of more than 20 miles – but shorter for the women – demanding accurate navigation, especially on a day like this, in the roughest country. This year's course went over, or near, the widely-scattered summits of Crag Hill, Dale Head, Seathwaite Fell and Red Pike with a dozen valleys deeply scored between them. In a race, in appalling weather, with perspiration running into your eyes, your body shivering with cold and the map streaming with water, which way would you go through the boiling cloud from, say, Crag Hill to Dale Head? There were problems like this all the way round, with thousands of feet to be climbed and much scree and rough ground to be descended, but most people got all the way round. The winner, a 22-year-old Borrowdale farm lad – his third victory in a row – did so in an incredible four and a quarter hours, nearly 25 minutes ahead of the second man. For this superb effort he holds a trophy for a year and picked up a piece of outdoor gear. This is real amateur sport at its finest – people competing for the fun (or love) of the game, not for money or the adulation of the crowd. The car park at the event, a quagmire before the end, was packed with cars – not of spectators, for this is not a spectator sport, but of competitors, most of whom had had to get up in the middle of the night and drive long distances to get to the start on time. In 40 years this annual event has never been cancelled, no matter what the weather, although one year, in even worse conditions than last week, it was slightly shortened. And there was one year, when it rained cats and dogs all day, when all the best runners in England were forced to retire, leaving one Lancashire lad to finish on his own.

Buried in snow

❧ FEBRUARY 1996 ❧

The morning sunshine sparkled on the snow-crusted crags atop the east face of the Old Man until they looked like fairy castles in icing sugar. Only the fleecy contrails of an unseen aircraft high above Swirl How disturbed a completely cloudless, bright blue sky. In sheltered corners, the sun was pleasantly warm; elsewhere, a biting wind sweeping straight out of the east chilled us to the bone. Enjoying, the other day, our friendly battle with the wind and ice steps treacherously overlaid with snow, I remembered a different day on the same hill almost 65 years ago. The snow was the deepest I have ever seen in England – several feet deep and snowing hard all day, with blizzard conditions and no visibility whatsoever. We were a gang of young climbers on an 'off-day' from our huts near the lake shore for there was far too much snow for climbing. Everything was buried deep in snow – all the tracks, spoil heaps, quarry huts, machinery, even small crags – but we ploughed blindly on, up any likely-looking slope, taking turns at the exhausting job of trail-breaking. None of us knew where we were until, all at once, we saw Low Water just below us. The other day this lovely mountain tarn was frozen right across, looking fit for skating. On this long-distant day, it was piled high with huge ice-floes and looked like a corner of Spitzbergen. Cutting across the flank of the mountain to avoid crags, we suddenly disappeared one by one into what seemed a hole in the ground; we had fallen through the roof of a buried quarrymen's hut and, at last, had a respite from the blizzard and a chance to eat our frozen sandwiches. The rest of the day's adventures will take too long to tell – how we found the summit, our descent down icy slopes to Goats Water – but I well remember how, at the end of the day, we peeled off our outer garments, frozen stiff as mediaeval armour, stood them up against the wall of our hut, and photographed them.

The power of storms
DECEMBER 2000

Watching the swollen River Kent racing through Kendal the other day one could only feel relief that Lakeland has, largely, escaped the serious flooding that has hit other places. I wrote 40 years ago that the floods of 2 November 1898 were probably Lakeland's worst in living memory. The level of Windermere was so high, you could row right across Belle Isle which was completely submerged, and craft in boathouses around Bowness Bay rose on floodwaters until they were bumping against the ceilings. Langdale was one huge lake, buildings at the gunpowder works were swept away, bridges were destroyed in Patterdale, Coniston and Kendal, the water was

6ft deep on some roads, and the main road from Grasmere to Keswick was completely wrecked and piled high with boulders washed down the fellsides. Something similar, but on a much smaller scale, happened recently, but in 1898 the main road was impassable for months; the 'new' road on the western side of Thirlmere had to be used. I remember the cloudburst that broke over the upper slopes of Wansfell one June afternoon in 1953, bucketing nearly two-and-a-half inches of rain on to Ambleside within three hours. Hailstones fell as big as pigeons' eggs, huge trees were torn out by their roots, boulders crashed down fellsides, floods carved out new ravines, wrecking walls and roads, and a holiday visitor was washed to his death. Seathwaite in Borrowdale staged the wettest Lakeland day ever – 8.03in on 12 November 1897 – and the tiny hamlet can claim eight of the ten wettest days in England in the last one hundred years.

Autumn on the way
❧ OCTOBER 2001 ❧

The full russet glory of the dying bracken has yet to clothe the fells and the colours in the woodlands have barely changed, but already the hills have about them the quiet resignation of autumn. Pale shafts of tired sunlight slant through the passes on still afternoons of long, blue shadows and blurred skylines, and in many a north-facing corrie winter feels not far away.

In the dales there is a new quiet after the brief bustle of summer, and you sniff woodsmoke from the first fires in the cottages for months. At home, the River Kent, in new, welcome spate after the first rain for weeks, races through Kendal, sweeping the mindless litter of bedsteads, shopping trolleys and traffic cones out to sea, and the equinoctial gales redden the cheeks and bring out the anoraks.

Sometimes the Lake District seems to move into autumn almost overnight, so that you wake up one morning to discover that new, warm colours of yellow, orange and red have been painted while you slept – and this is almost happening now. They are still water-skiing on Windermere and the ice-cream man remains on daily duty on White Moss Common, but small boys have already started hauling bonfire material along the lanes.

But this is going to be a sadder autumn than most – the fears of conflict abroad and, locally, the still-growing scourge of foot-and-mouth. I look out of my windows at the surrounding fells – the Howgills, the Whinfell ridge, the Scout Scar tops, Potter Fell, Benson Knott. All, after many long months, still out of bounds – and, except for Ingleborough, all the Yorkshire dales as well. Glorious autumn has, for once, lost its savour.

A double glory
✍ MAY 2003 ✍

The glorious, spring weather with the fells shouting to be explored made my inability to get out, for a variety of reasons, even more difficult to endure. In compensation, I've been recalling great moments in the hills – not just the obvious ones such as the first ascent of a particularly difficult climb or a near-miraculous survival epic in winter, but ordinary, everyday delights that anyone can enjoy. Like sunrise from the top of Helvellyn with the flaming gold of dawn suddenly flashing over the Northern Pennines, or perhaps the dying sunset, from Red Screes, sinking behind the blue-black Scafells and the first lights of evening twinkling in the valley far below. Many people have enjoyed the sight, from the high fells, of the whole of Lakeland apparently covered in a sea of cotton-wool, with the tops of the highest peaks peeping out like islands, and, from the top of Scafell at dawn, I've seen England, Scotland, Ireland

and the Isle of Man, seemingly quite close, and, across the sea, the mountains of North Wales.

But one of my most memorable summit experiences was once reaching the top of Bowfell, in deep snow, to find the sun shining on the sea of cotton wool, with only the tops of the Scafells showing above it, and, turning round, seeing a superb Brocken Spectre circled with a double 'glory'. It was the seventh or eighth Brocken Spectre I'd seen but the very first with a double 'glory'. But the everyday experience of clouds in the hills and the dale leaping up at you from far below as the mist is blown away is always memorable. And so is the sight of harebells by a mountain pool or the view, say, of Ullswater from Keldas.

Snow business
DECEMBER 2003

While I was knocking this out on my laptop a week ago, the sun was blazing down out of a cloudless sky on the Bannisdale hills and the Whinfell range so clearly I could see every stone on Kendal Castle just across the river. There was the slightest dusting of snow on the very highest fells, but it only lasted an hour or two. Where have all the winters gone? They say the snow is deserting the Alps, that Scottish skiing, declining for years, may not last much longer, while good Lakeland winters are becoming little more than happy memories.

Surprisingly, the ski tow on Raise near Helvellyn was in use for 10 days last season, but 30 or 40 years ago we could count on up to four months of skiiing almost every winter. Out in the hills every winter weekend we always had skis, boots and ice-axes in the car – just in case. And, if we were going to the northern Pennines, say Great Dun Fell, we also carried an old carpet, a bag of sand (for weight on the rear wheels) and a shovel – to keep moving on snow-bound roads. I've skied on Raise in May and, one year, some enthusiasts did a token ski run on the skirts of Cross Fell on mid-summer's day. And I've kicked steps up frozen snow in Central Gully, Great End in late June, watched children snowballing on the top of Helvellyn in September and witnessed one year when snow was lying somewhere in the fells on every month.

Then, there's skating – the memorable winter 74 years ago when I skated for miles along frozen Windermere, and dozens of outings on Rydal Water, Tarn Hows and the rest. Everything's changing – not just the weather but the seasons. Can we really dream this year of a white Christmas?

CHAPTER SEVEN

Battles and Bugbears

THE LAKE DISTRICT is breathtakingly beautiful but it has never been a paradise where contented dalesfolk lead privileged lives remote from the dirt and noise of towns. Like the rest of the British countryside, Harry Griffin's beat was constantly beset by threats, rows and sometimes real disasters. He recorded every extreme of weather and the resulting chaos, as well as two outbreaks of foot-and-mouth disease. The *Guardian* wanted its Country Diarists to reflect these things as well as the loveliness of Nature. In the words of the writer Geoffrey Moorhouse, who as a *Guardian* reporter marked the diarists' change from initials to full names in April 1966, the little band was manning one of the world's busiest and most interesting frontiers, between the environment (as the world's green spaces were just starting to be called) and the advance of technology, for good and ill.

As befitted a retired lieutenant colonel, Harry was extremely active on this frontier, not just as a journalist but in a bewildering number of civic roles. If his family sometimes felt that they had a rival in the fells, they also had to give up their husband and father to committees and associations of every sort. He was on the access and accommodation committee of the Lake District planning board, the youth committee and unemployment committee of Westmorland County Council, the committees of the Lake District's Naturalists Trust, Mountain Trials Association and Ski Club and those of Kendal's Civic Society, Rotary Club and Abbeyfield Society for housing the elderly. On the last, at least, he worked with Mollie who was a great Abbeyfield volunteer and tower of strength.

None of these positions were collected as trophies; Harry was passionate about the issues involved. He showed this in the way he flung himself into unofficial campaigns such as battles against reservoirs where he was very much on the opposite side from the Establishment. The *Guardian* was a suitable platform for these. Although the staunchest promoter of Manchester from its earliest days, it had demanded more parks rather than factories as long ago as 1844. It had also been happy to discomfort the city fathers with campaigns such as The Need for More Fresh Air. And in 1911 Canon H.H. Rawnsley, one of the founders of the National Trust, launched a blistering attack on the Lord Mayor of Manchester in the *Guardian*, after the mayor rashly claimed that John Ruskin would have liked the hideous trimmed laurels, Welsh slate and Scottish granite of the civic waterworks buildings at newly flooded Thirlmere.

Harry's most vigorous and successful campaigns were against similar proposed flooding in the Winster valley and reservoir plans for both Windermere and Ullswater. He was an able committee man, understanding the arguments of the thirsty Lancashire conurbations but relentless in making the stronger case for some of the most unspoilt scenery in the country. One of his fellow former pupils at Barrow secondary school was the famous advocate Norman Birkett, later Lord Birkett, and the two men met again at the Buck

Ruxton murder trial which Harry covered for the *Lancashire Evening Post*. Birkett denied Harry's claim that he had carved his name on a school desk – the one Harry used after him – but his oratory and powers of persuasion in court made a great impression on the young journalist. They were to team up in the 1950s in opposition to the reservoirs, and Harry always enjoyed seeing the lawyer's name chiselled on the rock summit of Birkett Fell above Ullswater, named in his honour because of his battling for the Lakes (more successful than his defence of Ruxton, who was hanged).

It was harder for Harry to retain the calm reasoning of a barrister when it came to defending the Lake District against another threat: the excesses of mass tourism. There was nothing new about this; indeed the organized train excursions and charabanc outings of the early twentieth century exceeded in numbers the visitors who came by car until well into the 1970s. You still pass the ruins of the old Easedale Tarn refreshment hut beyond Sour Milk Gill, a place where a building of any sort would be inconceivable today. But modern tourism seemed to Harry to bring far more litter and thoughtlessness than in the past, more potentially damaging technology such as schemes for chairlifts and revolving mountain restaurants and even, harmless though they might seem to less experienced walkers, a great too many cairns.

He was an unstinting admirer of P.J.H. Unna, founder of the Gadarene Club, whose members removed more than 300 'unnecessary' waymarking cairns – small piles of stones built up by passing ramblers – from a mere six fells. He was publicly very cross when he walked over Nan Bield pass and counted 128 cairns along the route, which is not hard to follow even in mist. When walkers did get lost, however, another of Harry's public works was to give them a hand in getting back on track. Although too busy to be a permanent member of a fell rescue team, he often sorted out the human equivalent of cragfast sheep, as he engagingly describes in the diary of November 1982 in which he reunites a mist-befuddled walker with his lost girlfriend. He seems to have had less success in restoring a vandalized plaque in memory of one Caroline Kimberley to her family. The only surviving response was from a reader who had found and hastily rehidden an unmarked tin of ashes in the scree nearby.

Markings on the map were central to yet another campaign, which he lost: the doomed fight to save Westmorland from the wholesale change of English local government in 1974. Much the most frequent date line on Harry's diaries had been 'Westmorland', and he never forgave the disappearance of the county, his own favourite and, he considered, the most beautiful in the country. He lamented that his view of four counties from his bungalow at Cunswick End had been cut at a stroke to just two; from Cumberland, Westmorland, Lancashire and Yorkshire, to Yorkshire and the new conglomerate, Cumbria. In a more practical way, he felt that the intensely local loyalties developed over centuries towards the small and ancient shire would take years to develop for Cumbria. He stuck to his *Guardian* dateline of 'Westmorland' for five years after the change, to annoy the authorities.

There were other battles, against the felling of ancient trees (something which also enraged Canon Rawnsley at Thirlmere), and the flipside of that issue – too many conifers planted for forestry in dark regiments along the dales. But Harry was a conservationist rather than a conservative. Just as he greatly approved of *Bluebird*, whose engines were noisy but quieter than quarry blasting, and the Sunderland flying boats made on Windermere during the Second World War, so he was delighted to find Lake District air on sale in souvenir tins. Just a pity, he said, that the entrepreneur who had this bright idea came from London rather than the 'old, grey town' of Kendal.

Orange peel
❧ APRIL 1954 ❧

It is a sober commentary on the British way of life that the National Trust has to spend £250 a year picking up litter on its properties in the Lake District. People presumably visit these places to drink in the especial beauty of the scene, but apparently they leave them more or less covered in orange peel, bits of paper, cigarette packets and – an increasing menace – camera film cartons. It is a relief to discover that the Trust is not greatly inconvenienced by empty bottles but it is very conscious of the near indestructibility of orange peel and the durability and brightness of the snapshotters' rubbish. Men are actually employed to go the round of the 'beauty spots' picking up litter, while presumably those equally delightful places which have not yet been 'discovered' by the tourist are as yet untainted by decaying ham sandwiches and the almost imperishable greaseproof paper in which they were wrapped. Even the popular mountain summits are occasionally visited by properly accredited scavengers and one of the places needing most attention is Scafell Pike itself. Even higher than 3000 feet above sea level a piece of orange peel will last, it is thought, about six months and still make a glitter among the boulders. Banana skins are viewed with less disfavour for they lose their colours in an hour or two and disintegrate quickly – but unfortunately few bananas are taken on to the fells. Dry stone walls seem to be a favourite repository for the unwanted contents of luncheon baskets, while a thaw always brings to light unsavoury relics once stupidly buried in the snow.

War games
ᴥ MARCH 1959 ᴤ

Four jet fighters, rather like children's darts, dived out of the haze at
500mph, pumping 30mm cannon shells into a lonely stretch of
Westmorland fellside, which, five minutes earlier, had been blasted
by tanks, artillery, machine guns and mortars. Yet two or three
hundred yards away, sheep, stolidly grazing on their centuries-old
'heaf' [the part of the fellside which is their native home], did not
even bother to lift up their heads at the din, so accustomed have they
become to the noise of battle. It is now many years since twelve
farms near this northern backbone of England were taken over by the
War Department so that tank men could be taught gunnery, and this
pleasant area of rocky hills and rolling moors is now the biggest thing
of its kind in the country. The sheep still graze on the higher slopes
and, as even Westmorland stone walls do not last long when there is
H.E. [high explosive] flying about, they are often to be found
among the shell craters on the range as well. Their indifference to the
explosions is quite remarkable. During this week's 'battle', in which
150 soldiers took part – watched by 500 officers – they were not
even perturbed by small pieces of the countryside raining down
upon them. Apparently a few of the boldest perish each year but not
nearly so many as those who die of disease or by falling over crags.

Des res
ᴥ JULY 1955 ᴤ

The value of old stone barns, shippons or decrepit farm buildings
in many a Lakeland valley must have jumped up spectacularly in
recent years – not their value for hay storage or as cattle shelters
but for living in. Dozens of old, tumbledown places have become

comfortable climbing huts, pleasant week-end cottages, or even commodious permanent residences since the war and the demand seems to be as great as ever. Perhaps the improvement grants being offered by local authorities have something to do with this urge to get away from the towns and settle down – even with oil lamps – among the fells. These new countryfolk from the cities seem to balance, ironically enough, the 'drift from the land', the itch of many a youngster brought up in the dales to get out into the world of motorcycles, cinemas and dance halls. And so, although the dale heads may look a little tidier in places, the folk are maybe different.

The prospect of new arrivals in the dale will be a topic of conversation for weeks ahead. 'I see old Tom's place's gone at last. Chap from Preston, they say. The roof's bad and it's a terrible cold spot, but I believe old Tom soaked him for it. Wonder if they've any kids?'

This last is an important point. Two or three more children might make all the difference to the fate of the tiny village school and mean more playmates for the other children, more trade at the village shop, and even more work for the bus-driver, the doctor or the parson. Unlike those terrible holiday boarding houses, where children are not wanted, these tiny rural communities will be glad of as many as they can get.

Invaders in paradise
❧ MAY 1956 ☙

There will be thousands of visitors to the Lake District this week-end. How many will be able to behave themselves? At Easter time hooligans burned down a litter box in Westmorland's loveliest valley and scattered the contents, including bottles and tins, about the fellside. They are also reported to have danced in triumph around the smouldering remains of a farmer's gate which they had set on fire, torn down walls, broken into barns, threatened the dalesfolk with violence, and departed without paying camping dues. Perhaps things are not quite so bad as this every weekend but they can be bad enough to keep decent folk away from popular valleys at holiday time. Most of the offenders are young people who have arrived by motor coach, bus or motorcycle; they come from the towns and they bring the worst habits of the towns to the dales. There have also been recent complaints around here about the nuisance caused by certain badly-organized motor trials – motorists speeding dangerously along narrow country lanes, driving without permission across farm land, backing into private gardens and generally annoying the residents. The litter nuisance goes on unabated and here perhaps we are all to blame, locals and visitors, young and old, the motorist and the walker. Hooliganism can be stamped out by the police but the litter problem needs an enlightened campaign, perhaps spread over years.

March of the overhead wires
❧ FEBRUARY 1961 ☙

Three days ago in a lovely Cumberland valley, they argued for seven hours about whether or not forty-four poles should be erected to carry electricity to the head of the dale; yesterday in a Westmorland valley on the other side of the Lake District, they were arguing about whether the wooden poles which have decorated the dale for years should be left alone or taken down. Much ado about nothing? Well, it depends on how high you set your standards. A few poles and a bit of wire may not completely ruin a lovely landscape but they may well spoil perfection – just as would the thinnest pencil line ruled across an Old Master. The tragedy about these cases is, of course, that while the engineers and the perfectionists carry on with their wrangling, the locals have to put up with their oil lamps

– a high price to pay, they claim, for living in paradise. It should all have been settled so very long ago. Had there been agreement twenty, or even ten, years ago that certain areas should not be spoiled by overhead cables – the extra cost of undergrounding being rightly met by the nation – whereas in other areas they could be allowed, everybody would have been happy. But now we continue to go to the expense of these dreary public inquiries and, in February 1961, spend hours arguing about whether Borrowdale is really a beautiful valley and whether Baddeley's superlatives were really necessary. 'Let there be light,' said the last speaker at the inquiry just before we stumbled out of the village hall into darkest Borrowdale and drove towards the distant bright lights of Keswick.

Second homes
JUNE 1964

The pretty little cottage farther up the dale with the rather striking modern curtains and the gleaming car in the pebbly drive is neither a quarryman's house nor the home of a local farm worker or forester. It is now owned by 'off-comers' – nice people who come up nearly every weekend and spend several weeks in the summer time, pottering about the country in their old tweeds and sensible shoes. There are scores of these weekend or holiday cottages scattered about the district and they are presenting a very real problem. For the local working folk, just married or perhaps looking out for a little place for their retirement, cannot compete with the money these 'off-comers' are prepared to give for an old cottage suitable for conversion. And so every half-derelict cottage bought by an 'off-comer' contributes to the drift of the local folk away from the countryside.

Too many of the disheartened young dalesfolk are being forced to seek their fortunes in the cities while the valleys are filling up with the elderly and the comparatively well-to-do. And gradually the flavour of some of the dales is changing. One cannot blame the 'off-comers' – real lovers of the area, most of them, and more knowledgeable about it, too, than many of the locals – but it must be admitted that as a community they do not always contribute a great deal to the life of the district. But an attempt is being made to face up to the problem by one non-profit-making society which is acquiring old cottages and smartening them up – entirely for local people. Some of their conversions have been beautifully done and as a result of the society's foresight quite a few of the dalesfolk have been enabled to live out their lives in their own countryside.

Fighting the flooders
MAY 1966

Half a dozen of us sat in a bright, low-raftered room at the back of a pleasant white-washed inn that looks out across an old bridge to the fells. Damson and cherry blossom beckoned through the windows and we could hear a curlew mournfully quartering a stubble field and, now and then, the persistent cuckoo. But no other sounds this sunny spring morning – not even the swish of cars on the gravel. We were meeting in committee to discuss the future of the long wooded valley that winds southwards from the inn past scattered farmsteads and old houses, nestling in folds in the tilled land. Two years ago, right out of the blue, we heard that all this quiet loveliness might be turned into a reservoir to supply water to a city 100 miles away. If that should happen the inn, with all the rest of this old-world hamlet and perhaps 50 farms scattered down the valley, will disappear.

Many times in this last two years we have sat in this back room with our agenda papers and pencils trying to hammer out the case for the people we represent – 216 people whose lives will be changed for ever should this tragedy descend on the valley, and hundreds of thousands of people all over England who love this unspoilt corner of the fell country. But nobody will wipe out our fears, the sword still hangs on its thread over our heads, and yesterday we heard that the city is to take over two more of our lakes. We got through our agenda this morning and made our plans but how frustrating it all seems. Why cannot the Water Resources Board or the Ministry come out into the open and say, firmly and finally, 'We won't flood the Winster Valley and we have torn up the plans'? Surely this valley is more important than anybody's convenience?

Foot-and-mouth strikes
NOVEMBER 1967

If the public have hearkened to press, radio and television appeals or obeyed the courteous requests of wardens at the foot of the fell paths, the mountains will have been quieter this weekend than during the war years. This is the first time in my memory that there has been no welcome in the hills, and it has taken a national emergency to bring it about. Climbing, walking, skiing, hunting, fishing and a dozen other pursuits and gatherings all stopped so that thousands of little grey sheep can have a chance to survive. For once the dread scourge got on to the unfenced fell farms, where the only boundaries are the 'heafs' of the Herdwicks, Roughs and Swaledales, it could spread like wildfire right up to the Scottish border, with appalling slaughter to follow. The freedom of the fells is traditional and Lake District landowners almost always accommodating – even long-suffering at times. But now lovers of the open air have the chance to repay them for more than a century of patient tolerance – by just keeping away. My last memory of the fells, therefore, for some little time – apart from the sight of their familiar shapes from my windows – may be an early November walk along the tops that look northwards across the Brathay into Westmorland. It was a glorious morning with the last of the larch needles down in the ravine showing yellow in the sunshine, the becks in spate, a few specks of snow still clinging to the Scafells, and a shrill wind on the summit that kept you moving. And back in the dale in the late afternoon there were the fragrance of woodsmoke, the westering sun lighting up an old spinning gallery and the first shy buds of winter jasmine.

A golden dream of cable cars
⟋⟍ MARCH 1972 ⟋⟍

The Lancashire businessman who last year wanted us to put up cable-cars and sky-domes around Windermere has returned to the attack and again enjoins the Lake District to cash in on the 'pot of tourist gold' which, he claims, is just waiting to be picked up. He thinks we should 'roar into the seventies and eighties', accede to the demands of the 'majority' for proper facilities, attract as many people as possible to the national park – and make as much money out of them as we can. Once again this indefatigable writer of letters to the newspapers seems to have got his priorities all wrong. To him the Lake District is a playground to be exploited, not a beautiful, largely-unspoiled corner which must be safeguarded from increasing pressures if it is to remain the heritage for our grandchildren that was given into our care. One would have thought that the limit in people, motorcars, coaches and caravans has already been reached, in the short high season, in Bowness, Ambleside, and Keswick. Tourism for the fringe areas around the national park – places like North and East Westmorland, the Solway Coast and the Cumberland Plain – could well be a worthwhile objective, while the season should certainly be considerably extended to relieve the pressures in high summer on central

Lakeland. But to go all out to attract more visitors to the heart of the district by the provision of 'facilities' more proper to a seaside resort would be the greatest mistake.

Wiped off the map
◆ NOVEMBER 1974 ◆

On the same day that the infant Cumbria County Council acquired its new coat of arms, nearly 3000 copies of a little booklet, compiled in affectionate memory of the ancient county of Westmorland – wiped off the map by Whitehall early this year – were being distributed. The booklet, which traces the history of the former county since the days when the Stone Age men had their axe factory in the Langdale Pikes, has been sent to all former employees of the county council including road men, teachers and nurses – in gratitude for their services and to mark the end of 1000 years of the county's active history. Westmorland was, to many of us, the loveliest and least spoiled county in England, a county of sturdy independence and fine traditions, but the name does not even appear on the new maps. Reorganization, in the name of progress, spelled out the end and it is revealing to recall what Governor Petronius had to say about reorganization at the time when Nero was Emperor of Rome. 'A wonderful method for creating the illusion of progress while producing confusion, inefficiency and demoralisation.' This was nearly 2000 years ago but, as recently as 1965, the Local Government Commission came to the firm conclusion that 'Westmorland should not be disturbed' since it was 'unlike any other county in England'. But despite all this and a great deal of battling by many people, dear old Westmorland has now gone for ever, although the spirit of the Land West of the Moors will live on. And, at least, the College of Heralds have not forgotten Westmorland in the new Cumbria coat of arms. The old Herdwick ram of Westmorland still tops the crest and the red lion of Appleby is one of the supporters.

When the beauty was scarred
ᔬ AUGUST 1980 ᔭ

The dead-end valley of Newlands is one of the least-spoiled corners of the fell country – a quiet dale, untouched by the scars of tourism, of lonely, tree-sheltered farms, a little, white church and a long-winding beck below encircling heights carpeted with heather and bilberry. Nearly 50 years ago, with youthful optimism, I decided that some day I would retire to this idyllic backwater but, although the date has remained unchanged throughout my lifetime, events did not quite turn out that way. Newlands, though, is still a favoured retreat for quietude and seclusion – strange, when it is remembered that 200 or 300 years ago this was one of the busiest and most industrialized dales in Lakeland. Starting in the sixteenth century, German, Dutch and English miners, in successive enterprises, tore up the fellsides for copper, lead and other minerals, including some silver and even small quantities of gold so that the sleepy dale of today must then have been a thriving and populous place, ugly with the noise, excavations, erections and litter of industry. Nature and farming have long since healed the scars and only if you know where to look will you find the soil heaps, the ruined stone huts and the pony tracks zig-zagging up the fells. During a recent round of the heights from Little Town on a wet and misty day I pottered around three of the old mines and tried to picture the Newlands of long ago – before the first tourists came – when the valley meant hard labour for many and great wealth for the few. Goldscope mine – the name comes from Gottesgab or God's gift and not from the gold that might have been found there – was, in fact, last worked during the First World War.

Excuse me, I've lost my girlfriend
November 1982

A round of the Langdale fells, starting with Jack's Rake on Pavey Ark and finishing with the descent of Hell Gill, was enlivened by a curious encounter on Hanging Knotts. The day, for a change, had been clear with gusty winds on the tops but, after an interesting scramble through the crags above Rossett Gill, I emerged into thick cloud on the stormy plateau, quite close to Ore Gap. Almost at once I met another lone walker, picking his way in the direction of Esk Pike but, as he explained, hopelessly lost. Could I help, he asked. He had left his girlfriend below in the mist, after walking along something called The Belt, and had been trying to find her for the last hour without success. No, he had no compass. 'Could it have been The Band?' I asked and he thought that might have been the name, so I had to tell him that he was about a mile out of his way and going in the opposite direction. With obvious relief, he agreed to accompany me over Bowfell and eventually, some distance above Three Tarns, we found his companion who seemed to have weathered the wait with fortitude, despite the cold. There was a touching reunion. This young man was not the first to go astray in mist on the extensive Bowfell summit plateau – or in many places in the Lakeland fells in poor conditions. One wonders, indeed, how many casual walkers in the hills carry compasses and know how to use them. Accurate compass work is the most satisfying reward of a day in the clouds and a very necessary insurance. If regularly taught in schools compass navigation could save lives, avoid distress – and provide fun. And, despite reports to the contrary, compasses do work accurately on Bowfell – provided they are held in the hand and not placed, in certain places only, on the rock.

Memorial mystery
APRIL 1996

The high fells are dotted with memorials of one sort or another, from the splendidly-sited Robinson's Cairn near Pillar Rock to the well-known cluster on Helvellyn remembering a faithful dog, a foolhardy fox-hunter and an adventurous aeroplane landing. Elsewhere are memorials to poets, writers, conservationists, a foxhound – near Dow Crag and, on both sides of Sty Head Pass, the biggest memorial of all – the high fells above 1500ft given to the nation in memory of members of the Fell and Rock Climbing Club who died in the First World War. Altogether there are probably dozens of them, including bridges, crosses, cairns and memorial seats for admiring the view. But one of them, in a little rock shelter high up on the Breast Route just below the top of Great Gable, was new to me – until recently. Nowadays, I don't often go this way up Gable where, for some time, Ray McHaffie and his gang have been hard at work renewing the grievously-eroded track, preferring routes from the north or west, so I had not spotted this modest memorial. It consisted of a brass plaque, measuring about eight by six inches, cemented on to a boulder at the back of the shelter, and reading: 'In memory of Caroline Kimberley whose premature death in 1991 robbed her of her sole ambition to climb Great Gable.' I have no idea who this lady was or how or where she died: did she, perhaps, die on the mountain at this very place? But somebody will know and may be concerned when next they pass this way to find the plaque has disappeared. A friend of mine, who had seen the plaque on previous occasions, discovered on a recent visit that it had become detached and was lying in the scree some distance away. So, to preserve it for relatives or friends, he took it home for safe keeping. Anybody interested should contact me and I will be happy to give them his address and telephone number.

After the plague
JANUARY 2002

The dalesmen's sport, fox-hunting on the fells, is gradually returning after its 11-months' foot-and-mouth ban. Already the
Lunesdale pack which hunts the fells around Sedbergh has been in
action, and the Lakeland mountain packs are expecting to restart in
turn, subject to certain restrictions.

I've never been a hunting man, although I've stumbled upon
dozens of hunts in the fells and taken part in many a 'merry neet'
with hunting folk, even joining in the old choruses. But my
sympathies are with the fox, fleeing for his life with a score of
baying hounds chasing him through the crags, and I've always been
glad when he's escaped.

At the same time, I realize that foxes, whose numbers will have
increased during the hunting ban, must be kept down, and hunting
seems the most practical, and even the most humane, method,
especially in mountain country. You've got to be very fit to follow
the hounds on foot – rather than driving, with your binoculars, to
some convenient lookout point by car. I've always admired the skill
and mountain knowledge of the huntsmen and whippers-in, and
marvelled at the incredible fitness and dexterity in wild places of
the hounds.

The last hunt I came across was in the Mungrisdale fells at the
back of Blencathra. I told my companion we would have the hills to
ourselves but they were alive with noisy hunt followers, all with
their mobiles, and loud with the 'music' of the pack in full cry.
Lakeland hunting traditionally takes place when there's an 'r' in the
month, and a friend of mine uses this formula for eating porridge
at breakfast – never after April. Hound trailing fills in the summer
months.

Defender of the Lakes
SEPTEMBER 2003

A correspondent enquires about Symonds Knott, reportedly included in an extended Bob Graham round of Lakeland peaks [the Bob Graham Round, England's toughest fell-running challenge, involves scaling 42 peaks in 24 hours]. Where and what is it, he asks? Symonds Knott is, in fact, one of the highest and most dramatically-sited peaks in Lakeland – a rough pile of boulders, topped by a cairn, a few hundred yards north of the summit of Scafell, just above the great gulf of Deep Gill, looking across to towering Scafell Pinnacle. According to Nuttall's authoritative guide to the 'two-thousanders' of England, it is a separate peak by rising above its surroundings on all sides by at least 50ft, and has the impressive height of 3146ft – one of the 251 'mountains' of England. It was named in honour of the Revd H.H. Symonds, one of the most determined of the campaigners for a Lakeland national park and the founder of the Friends of the Lake District, who died in 1958. His ashes were scattered there by his daughter, who died earlier this year, and his closest friends and associates.

I knew Symonds quite well; a short, vigorous, white-haired man who fought like a tiger the water boards, the Forestry Commission and anybody trying to exploit his beloved Lake District, and hung on like a Lakeland terrier often against all the odds. He also wrote, more than 20 years before Wainwright, one of the best and most erudite guides to the Lakeland fells – and he was, of course, one of the original members of the Lake District Planning Board. We who love Lakeland owe a great deal to this aggressive but kindly Christian, who could tackle ministers of the crown and tie them up in knots to safeguard his dearly loved corner of England.

CHAPTER EIGHT

Family and Friends

HARRY GRIFFIN had a happy home life as a boy, knocking around Barrow in his blue pullover with his grazed knees, and he was keen to provide the same thing for his own family later on. Although he was often described as falling in love for life at 18, with rock-climbing and the fells, it was a little later, as a young reporter in Preston, that he met a local girl called Mollie Barker, an office worker in the town. 'Lovely and cheerful,' he called her and she smiles with the eagerness of youth from the summit of Cairn Gorm in a matching photo for one she took of Harry, the young mountain tiger, standing in the snow by the same cairn on the same climb. She never had any illusions that life as Mrs Griffin would take place on level ground and it duly didn't. Their home for most of their 50 years of married life was exactly on the 500ft contour, two miles from Kendal, in a bungalow at Cunswick End whose garden Harry defended ceaselessly, and to the entertainment of Country Diary readers, against ants, snails and marauding sheep and cows.

Before proposing to Mollie, Harry put her through a series of Action Woman tests, one of them going a great deal closer to both their endurance limits than he had planned. Two years before their marriage in 1937, he went burning up to Skye with her in a Morris Minor convertible which he bought for £42 in Preston. On the road to the isles, he notched up the exhilarating achievement of clocking over 6omph for the first time. It was a safer way of travelling than the 350cc Le Vack New Hudson motorbike he used to get to the Tigers' climbing hut at Coniston, but once he and Mollie reached the Cuillins, transport was confined to their own legs. Both of them were excited by their first, unforgettable sight of the Black Cuillin ridge, which is far spikier and more serrated than anything in England. They had also read of the famous inner lake of Loch Coruisk, the old caldera of the Cuillin volcano, from which there were steep scrambles up to the ridge and back to civilization down the other side.

In theory. A laconic Scots boatman dropped the pair off at Coruisk in drenching rain with an inadequate map and an epic followed of slogging through bogs, scrambling up blind valleys and dangling down precipices on Harry's hemp rope. The fact that it didn't end the affair proved the strength of the bond. The couple were married on 23 October 1937, returning for their honeymoon to Scotland, where they found that their hotel in Aviemore had burned down, and ending up in a cottage whose only other guest was a bishop.

Their son, Robin, was born in 1939 and daughter, Sandra, in 1944, and family holidays quickly fitted the pattern set by Harry's Tiger apprenticeship and forays with Mollie to Scotland. The Griffin tents, caravan and hostel stays took them for memorably spartan trips to Skye, Arran and the Cairngorms after suitable training at home in the Lakes. Harry's Country Diary reflections on when to introduce young people to the fells were prompted by his own mixed experience. Sandra insisted on walking, unaided, to the top of the 'Mrs Tiggywinkle mountain' Catbells at the age of two-and-a-half and Robin led an expedition including his grandfather, Arthur Griffin, up Coniston Old Man when he was five. But attempts to take both children rock-climbing when they were too young were misguided and ended in failure. At seven-and-a-half, Robin complained that holds on Middlefell Buttress in Langdale were too far apart and Sandra recalls clinging in tears to a rope on what the manuals irritatingly called a 'moderately difficult' climb. Mollie successfully counselled delay before further lessons, though 'yelling on moderates', Sandra ruefully recalls, became a family catchphrase.

As the children grew older, Robin at Heversham Grammar School near Kendal, and Sandra at Kendal Girls' High School, the sun seemed to shine more frequently on the family holidays and what Harry himself recalled as 'weeks of rain and interminable bog-trotting' faded into the past. He had a mountain day in a thousand traversing the Cuillin ridge with Robin, who also chose to go to the island on honeymoon with his wife Mary. But the standard of accommodation remained the same, including a gloomy hostel whose only other resident ate fish from a bucket, although bizarrely it also had a Steinway piano which Harry played. Just once, when, tormented by midges, Harry drove over the cooking pots at a campsite, the Griffins ended up in a comparatively luxurious hotel.

Work often intervened. Not just the demands of the Country Diary and the *Evening Post*'s weekly Lakeland notebook, neither of which ever missed an instalment, but also the inevitable crises of news reporting. Harry was cabled on one Scottish holiday to return to cover the loss of the Royal Navy submarine *Thetis*. In compensation, he could keep the children enthralled with tales of some of his gorier jobs. The family also had many interesting friends in the Lakes on whom Harry drew for character sketches, notably

The trademark pipe – invaluable for keeping midges away
(Denis Thorpe, courtesy of Guardian Newspapers)

Alfred Wainwright and, from an earlier generation, Geoffrey Abraham, who is the veteran climber profiled in the diary below from November 1964. Mollie meanwhile kept the family fed, warm and cared for and entertained, while working for many voluntary causes in Kendal. She was a founding figure in the local Abbeyfield Society, which provided homes for the elderly, the Women's Royal Voluntary Service, the friends of the local hospital and the Rotary Inner Wheel, which elected her president.

In October 1987, she and Harry celebrated their Golden Wedding. But within a year she was dead from cancer. Harry was devastated and beset in simple, practical terms. He was the first to admit that he could not boil an egg. He wrote to Peter Preston at the *Guardian*, 'I hope I will be given the strength to continue my Country Diary pieces but time will show.' It was a very hard time, and all the more remarkable that he did indeed keep the diaries coming, on time and to length. Sandra returned from overseas – her career as a teacher and then freelance writer and editor had taken her to Canada and the Far East – to help him find a new and manageable home. They eventually chose a flat at High Fellside in Kendal, steeply up Beast Banks overlooking the Howgills in the distance and 'the old grey town's' town hall clock right in front. 'Welcome to Colditz,' Harry told hearth-warming friends.

And then one day two years later, one of his pals, Canon John Hodgkinson, bumped into him into the town to be told, 'I've been transmogrified,' a word the canon looked up, and found to mean 'transformed in an unexpected and magical way'. The cause of this was Violet Macaulay MBE, a redoubtable local voluntary worker and civic activist who became Harry's second wife in 1989. Touchingly, she consulted his favourite editor at the *Guardian*, Jeanette Page, over some doubts in her family about the propriety of moving in with Harry before they were actually married. But then, devastatingly, she too was dead from a heart attack within five months of the wedding and although Harry gradually picked up his life again, a further dreadful blow lay in store. In August 1998, his son Robin died from a heart attack, completely unexpectedly, at the age of 58. Like a severe rock pitch, Harry felt, life didn't get easier as on you went. But as with the good times, the skipping up Catbells and the Scottish expeditions, he recounted it all.

Dog in the lead
NOVEMBER 1956

The dog took the children merrily up the track past the quarries and away to the top of the pass while we followed sedately in the rear. We never take him in the fells – he takes us. He seems to say: 'Let me show you my countryside. So much better than your stuffy towns.' The day was warm, clear and sunny but he was not interested in scenery – only in the rabbit holes, the dirty pools and the birds, who annoy him. He would clearly love to have chased sheep, too, but after looking longingly at them in the distance, he remembered his manners. Yesterday he was combed and brushed, but he splashed into the first dirty pool and then sat down in it. A moment later he was halfway down a rabbit hole and then away off up the steep bracken towards a grouse, croaking in the heather. On the top of the pass he lay on a rock in the sunshine, tongue out, tail wagging, watching a beetle toiling through the grass jungle. Below us, we could just pick out traffic crawling along a road, and there was the distant sea, and the lakes and the fells standing up around us in the afternoon sunshine, but all he was thinking about was his dinner. It had not been a hard day – he once climbed four mountains between breakfast and dinner – but on the way down he did no more than growl at a big dog, twice his size, in the farm yard. Normally he would have been very annoyed.

How not to put children off
JUNE 1958

What is the youngest age at which one may take to the hills? The other day, on the rocky summit of a 2500ft Lakeland mountain, we came upon a nine-month-old baby boy. He was lying in a weird-looking contraption, something between a box kite and a rabbit hutch, which was strapped to the back of his determined-looking father. A hundred feet down the ridge, on her way to the summit, was the mother with a two-year-old infant hanging, face outwards, from the straps of her rucksack. Neither child was taking any interest in the remarkable view and, indeed, both looked extremely bored. At intervals, the younger child yelled lustily, being apparently happiest when it was being jolted up and down in its cage, and strongly resenting its father's well-earned summit rest. I wondered whether these children would grow up to appreciate their parents' obvious love of the hills, or whether the effort had been wasted. My own daughter walked over Sty Head when she was two, but it was ten years later before she came to enjoy this sort of thing. We took my boy on his first rock climb at the age of seven but it was many years before he asked us to take him on another. Children, perhaps, should be encouraged to love the hills – in their own time and in their own way.

Besieged by cows
❧ AUGUST 1964 ❧

The intruders came in the early morning hours, perhaps an hour before we got up, and although we heard them we paid no attention, believing the noises to be the usual grunts and lowings from the cows in the field beyond the hedge. But when we looked out on the garden we saw a disheartening scene of destruction – two lawns trampled deep with hoof-prints and most of the kitchen garden consumed. first we had the snails, then the birds, then the rabbits, and we had even been prepared for deer, but now they were getting bigger, for these had undoubtedly been cows. Some hiker must have left open a gate two or three farms away – these had not been the Friesians from over the fence – and these clumsy beasts had wandered in and enjoyed perhaps their best meal for months. 'Must have been in half an hour at least,' said our farmer sympathetically, surveying the damage.

Of course, we had asked for it by leaving an undefended drive but what can you do when you have been waiting for wallers for more than a year? Now we rig a rope section across the gap at night, but whether this will turn determined animals who have sighted pastures new and smelled the distant aroma of ripening Brussels sprouts remains to be seen. Meanwhile, the immediate problem was how to patch up the damage and it took us three days of a short holiday earmarked for better things. Each hole was sifted by fork, new filling added here and there, some grass seed sown, and a great deal of pummelling, rolling and cutting tried. After a week things look better and perhaps the winter rains and frosts will complete the repairs, but two years' work has been spoiled – not to mention the almost total loss of our autumn and winter vegetables. For all they left us were the carrots and the beans – oh, and the horse-radish, which we don't like anyway.

A first glimpse of Wainwright...
APRIL 1957

The guide writer spends his working life among files and ledgers at an office desk, but every free hour he is striding over the fells. He is not greatly concerned with valleys and lakes but only with the contours and all that they conceal. Every mountain and hillside must be quartered, measured, photographed and explored, every faint track followed and recorded, each beck traced to its source and each waterfall, cairn, tarn, quarry and sheepfold tracked down and sketched. He has spent many patient hours on lonely summits waiting for a gap in the clouds to expose the view and on many a wild, wet afternoon he is poking about in long-forgotten mine workings or searching for some old spring. Down from the fells in the evening the task goes on in the quiet of his study. Working with pen and indian ink he painstakingly prints out his text, draws his maps and panoramas, and sketches his illustrations. A night's careful toil might yield two-thirds of a page, but each evening for four years the work has gone on. This week the second of his two volumes has emerged from the publishers – each page an engraving of his own original work without one word of type, even to the cover. It is one man's way of giving thanks for the great joy which can come from the hills.

. . . and the last
ℜ JANUARY 2004 ℜ

Fifty years ago I was living in a Kendal stone-built house with a front lawn that sloped steeply down to the main Keswick road. Outside my garden gate was a bus stop and, every Saturday or Sunday morning, for two or three years, the borough treasurer could be seen by this gate waiting for the Keswick bus.

Alf, as I knew him – Mr Wainwright to most other people – was doing his last fellwalks before completing the first of his now-famous seven-volumed *Pictorial Guide to the Lakeland Fells*. For his earliest walks he had no mountain boots, just town shoes, and no anorak. He usually wore a lightweight macintosh and his flat cap. He didn't carry a compass and had no idea how to use one. If I was going in the fells I would sometimes offer him a lift but he would never accept. He seemed to enjoy travelling on buses but would never chat to the other passengers. Two or three times I took Wainwright out – when he asked me. The only other person to accompany him when he was doing the Lakeland guides was a Kendal bank manager whom he met on the bus and Alf, finding they were going to the same fell, surprisingly agreed to his company.

Wainwright was one of the clumsiest walkers you could meet –

unable to climb a stone wall – but showed great courage in his lone ascent of places such as Jack's Rake on Pavey Ark and the steep front of Grasmoor End. And his exploration of remote fells, far from buses, in all weathers, without a compass, was similarly courageous. Alf finished his first guide in 1954 and it was published, to widespread acclaim, in May 1955. Undoubtedly, Alf, who wrote 50 other books, was a genius.

Old man of the mountains
NOVEMBER 1964

An old man of 93 sits contentedly, surrounded by his mountain pictures and his memories, in a room that looks out over one of the finest views in England. He is the last living link with the deer-stalker-and-Norfolk-jacket-pioneers who founded the sport of mountaineering in this country and the man who first popularized the sport with his photographs and writings. For not only did he take his heavy plate camera into desperate places to picture deter-mined-looking men hanging on to rocks by their eyebrows, but he also found new ways up vertical crags in Scotland and Wales as well as his native Cumberland. And there is even a jagged aiguille high above Chamonix that bears his name. Remarkably, his memories of adventurous days 50, 60, even 70 years ago are almost as sharp today as the wonderful photographs that line the walls of his home. He even remembers his very first climb – Pillar Rock by the old Slab and Notch with the help of his mother's clothes line. 'There were some Alpine Club men on the Rock that day,' he recalls, 'and they were very kind and helpful and didn't laugh at our silly rope. I thought, "What wonderful men!" and decided to become a climber.' And he remembers, as if it was last year, his first discovery of a new route – a wet, vegetatious gully in the hills to the east of Keswick. 'There was a steep bit about half-way up with a waterfall streaming down, and I had a drink before tackling it. But when I pulled myself over the top, I found a dead sheep lying in the water and the next day I was very sick.' He was still climbing at 70, but today he can only lift his eyes to the hills that have been his whole life.

Farewell to Violet
❧ MARCH 1991 ❧

Our last little walk together was five days before she passed away. Disabled and walking with a stick, she couldn't go very far but she had an ambition to reach Loughrigg Terrace again. It was a crisp, sunny afternoon with ice on the track and streaks of snow on the tops. She struggled on bravely from the White Moss car park, across the bridge and up the rise, stopping now and again to look at the expanding view. At the last stop a robin alighted at our feet, suddenly appearing out of nowhere as robins do, and Violet talked to it. The robin, bright red, perky and friendly, accompanied us up the track. Every time we stopped, the robin stopped and he and Violet had another chat. We reached the start of the Terrace and the first patches of snow. She had made it. There was a chill east wind and we decided to go down, a painful process for Violet, balancing across the icy bits with her stick, and me chivvying and bullying her along in my usual fashion. I think I pointed out the views, identifying the tops, but she wouldn't have taken it all in. She wasn't that good at remembering Lakeland mountain names, mixing up Caw with Cow and talking of Stickling Pike. We reached the place where we had last seen the robin and there he was again. Suddenly he hopped on to my outstretched arm and Violet had a long chat with him, her face a foot from his beak. Finally we ambled down to the car. It had only been a little walk, barely a mile, but Violet said she had enjoyed it immensely. A week later, rearranging her possessions and trying to decide which of three large flower pots to retain, her friend told me: 'She always liked that one with the red robins on it. She loved robins.' So I kept that one and it now stands halfway up the stairs, full of her favourite flowers with the little red robin peeping out.

Failing as a mountain guide
MAY 1993

It was rather thoughtless of me to drag my daughter and son-in-law, badly jet-lagged by the long flight from Taiwan, up Helvellyn by the dreary trudge from Wythburn but quite inexcusable to take them down the rough, untracked way by the old lead mines, one of the most disagreeable descents in the district. Whelpside Gill, an enjoyable way up or down, especially, with its foaming beck and waterfalls, on a hot day, would have been much easier and far more pleasant but, from Brownrigg Well, the mines route looked an interesting challenge and I had forgotten its horrors – especially for people inured to the soporific humidity of Taipei and unaccustomed to using their legs. Certainly I will never come down this way again but my reputation as a mountain leader is now in ruins. Helvellyn is much more familiar to me in winter and I had forgotten the summer crowds on the popular routes. At least there was nobody else in the lead mines gill; does anybody ever go this way nowadays? Two days later the holiday visitors, still stiff from their ankle-shattering descent, refused to contemplate anything more strenuous than lovely Farleton Fell – even on another perfect morning. The familiar shape of Ingleborough bulked hugely in the east, across the white wrinkled foreground of limestone pavements, but the main interest was in the hang-gliders, parked near the cairns on the lower summit just above the busy A6. The pilots patiently explained the intricacies of the game to us before taking off into the gusty wind for a demonstration. One moment they were balanced on the edge of the drop, trying to steady the ungainly-looking wings, the next, they were soaring upwards like dragonflies on the strong thermals and then circling for half an hour in carefree abandon, seemingly without effort, the world far below their feet. We admired their skill and envied them their easy command of the skies. I recalled another recent encounter – walking down Ingleborough near Crinan Bottom when a man with a parachute on his back suddenly dropped out of the skies and landed at our feet, having jumped off the summit a few moments earlier. 'Far more exciting than walking down,' he told us, as he stuffed his parachute in his rucksack. Suddenly I felt quite old.

Bagging the 2000-footers
❧ JANUARY 1998 ❧

Up to three years ago my daughter-in-law, Mary, had never climbed any hill, anywhere. But last Monday, in the drizzle and low cloud that has bedevilled these parts for weeks, she completed the ascent of all the 280 or so two-thousanders in England by climbing Mickle Fell (2591ft), the highest summit in Durham. The collection of the 33 summits in the northern Pennines, under the appalling conditions that prevailed for most of the time, proved unexpectedly difficult, with much of the way trackless and navigation by compass essential. My son, Robin, unfamiliar with any of the terrain outside the Lakes and Yorkshire, led throughout but, after weeks of bog-trotting through driving rain or thick cloud, is now looking forward to a more restful period – climbing in the Himalayas in April. Several summits and, especially, Mickle Fell, lie within the the Warcop Artillery Range, with severely restricted access, many Danger Areas marked on maps, and stern warning notices at the entrances to the range: 'Danger W. D. Range. Shelled area. Beyond this point you proceed at your own risk.'

Having done their research and established that the only day of the week when firing was unlikely was Monday – not the ideal day for the average mountain-walker – they drove to the Cumbria-Durham boundary on the Brough to Middleton-in-Teesdale road and, sure enough, the red flag was tied down, indicating 'No firing'. In the thick cloud little was seen of the mountain, except the long line of boundary stones, a foot or so high – all marked on the map – that are a useful guide in bad weather, and the huge cairn – one of the biggest, they say, in England – on the sprawling summit plateau. On the way to their last mountain, beyond Kirkby Stephen, they had had a brief vision of sunlight on a distant sighting of new snow on Mallerstang Edge before the clouds came down and the interminable drizzle.

Old and young
❧ APRIL 1998 ❧

There were patches of ice on Wetherlam Edge and a flurry of hail as we scrambled up, but the clouds were high and the Scafells and half the Lakeland hills were startlingly clear. But not much sunshine. Indeed, for much of the afternoon, the only sunlit fells were Helvellyn and Dollywaggon, with the western slopes showing the only considerable snow on any of the tops. Clearly, there would be much more of it on their shadowed eastern slopes. Wetherlam, 'the mountain of a hundred holes', had always been one of our favourite hills when, 22 years ago, I sadly scattered the ashes of my brother near the summit. The place of pilgrimage is a rock corner in a splendid situation with Little Langdale and the Brathay countryside, splashed with many glittering waters, immediately below and, six miles away to the north-west, the ramparts of the Scafells. By the cairn this time were a couple with their grandson, Daniel, aged nine, who had come over Great Carrs and Swirl How – with Wetherlam, the lad's first two-thousanders. We wished him a lifetime of mountains. To return we wandered down the south ridge and Lad Stones to the old quarry track, past old copper mine workings, and down the side of Tilberthwaite Gill. The waterfalls in the gill were impressive enough but I remembered a day 50 years ago when two of us, for the adventure, climbed down the ravine, with all the waterfalls, when the gill was in lively spate, coming ashore on the shingle at its foot like a couple of drowned rats. Another memory of Wetherlam, out of scores, is of a snow ascent when we broke through fog on to the summit to find the sun shining on a sea of cotton-wool mist covering the whole of Lakeland and, when we turned round, a perfect Brocken Spectre, seemingly only yards away, with a rare double 'glory'.

Remembering a brother
❧ OCTOBER 1998 ❧

When we used to go over Birker Moor from the Duddon to Eskdale in the 1930s we noticed some crinkly rocks high up on a hill to the right and saw, from the map, that this was Great Worm Crag. 'A curious name,' we thought, 'we'll go up there some day,' but we never did. And, during the next 60 years or so, we often spotted the crinkly shapes, south-west of the more imposing Crook Crag and Green Crag, a couple of miles or so from Harter Fell, and decided: 'That must be Great Worm Crag.'

The other day, bright and sunny, we thought we'd take a look at the place and drove up the steep, winding hill from Ulpha. Sixty years ago the pleasant house at the foot of the hill used to be a hotel, the Travellers' Rest, and I remembered my brother and I, after a long day on the tops, going in there for a meal and, at the end of it, discovering we'd no money. But those were more trusting days, and the landlord accepted our promise to send the money as soon as we got home – which, of course, we did.

The ascent of Great Worm Crag, by a circuitous route embracing several little crags, proved undemanding although boggy, but the views from the summit of most of the Lakeland tops, and bits of Galloway, were quite superb. One of the best viewpoints in the district, we decided, and well worth the wait. Of course, we saw nobody on the round, the only movement being the occasional flash of a car going along the lonely fell road past Devoke Water. The lovely Duddon valley hasn't changed a scrap in 60 years – apart from the trees on Harter Fell. And now, I notice, they're cutting some of these down.

A devastating blow
❧ AUGUST 1998 ☙

My staunch companion in a lifetime of mountain days has, with shattering suddenness, passed on. Before me is a photograph of him, aged five and a half, standing by the summit cairn on Coniston Old Man. The picture was taken by his grandfather, my father, whom Robin had taken up the mountain. A very sound and knowledgeable mountaineer, he read maps as easily as other people read books or newspapers; with him you never got lost. When he was only 18, he and I traversed the Cuillin Ridge in Skye together – he was probably the youngest person to have done the ridge at that time. Earlier this year, Robin went on his first expedition to the Himalayas, to climb a peak of nearly 22,000ft. Out of a party of ten only four reached the summit, Robin, the oldest member, taking charge when the professional leader had to drop out with altitude sickness. He and I had enjoyed hundreds of wonderful days in the Lakeland fells, the Scottish hills, the Alps, the Yorkshire tops, the Northern Pennines. And, during the last three years, he had taken his wife to all the Lake District two-thousander summits and, eventually, to every summit in England. They were building a house in Kendal where they were planning to retire to devote the rest of their lives to the hills. Sadly, this is not to be.

Saying farewell
﹏ SEPTEMBER 1998 ﹏

The other day, warm with a pleasant breeze on the tops, I went back to Dow Crag, where I had started my climbing almost 70 years ago. But we weren't climbing this time, just walking over the top from Walna Scar to try to catch something of the flavour of those more adventurous days in the late 1920s. On the way we visited a secret place where, last month, we had sadly scattered the ashes of my only son, a fine mountaineer.

The modest ascent seemed more demanding than it used to be but the splendour of the view kept me going. For there are few ridges in Lakeland more rewarding than this one, with the long length of Dunnerdale, perhaps the least-spoiled valley in the area, stretched out far below and, straight ahead, the Scafells, the highest land in England with every tiny detail etched sharp against the sky.

From the top of one of the gullies on Dow Crag I looked down and watched two climbers on Trident Route, a well-remembered climb – the only two climbers we saw all day. Years ago there would have been dozens; perhaps climbers prefer quarries and climbing walls nowadays.

But scrambling about the summit and walking along the ridge were scores of people – from grannies (and at least one great-grandmother) to small children (including two babies in rucksacks) and several dogs. Other noticed changes were the grossly-eroded, stony tracks where there used to be grass, the growing profusion of unnecessary cairns and, above the fell-gate, more parked cars than I have ever seen there before.

Mountain-bikers on Walna Scar pass, and pony riders on the

lower slopes, added to the variety while, in the air, there were silent parascenders and buzzing microlights and, away to the south, a couple of balloons inching northwards, no doubt from Holker Hall. Big changes indeed, for, years ago, this used to be largely climbers' territory, but, happily, the beauty of these hills remains unchanged.

So that others may live
April 2000

The big RAF helicopter swung over the shoulder of the Old Man, swept across the dark pool of Goats Water and hung, hovering and shuddering like a giant kestrel, just above the screes below the great precipice of Dow Crag. Inside the aircraft, besides the crew and mountain rescue men, were Mary, my daughter-in-law, and myself, watching the installation of a new mountain rescue stretcher-box at the foot of the crag. The stretcher-box commemorates two climbers who were killed on the crag many years ago and now, also, my son Robin, who, inexplicably, died suddenly just 20 months ago – not long after a most successful expedition to the Himalayas. I happened to have been on the crag, as meet leader, when one of the climbers was killed through a breaking handhold and had had the sad task of informing his parents. Robin had first walked over Coniston Old Man and Dow Crag, with me, when four years old and, the following year, had proudly taken his grandfather, my father, completely unused to mountains, up the Old Man. In later years Robin climbed a great deal on Dow and other crags and, two days before his sudden passing, when we thought he was as splendidly fit as ever, took Mary, his wife, for a walk over the Old Man and Dow Crag. They had a great day and, on their way up, he had pointed out to Mary the blue blob of the stretcher box, at the foot of the crag. This old box, we later heard, was rotting away so a new stretcher-box, high up among Robin's very first and last hills, seemed an appropriate memorial. An earlier flight had lowered the box in a net to the foot of the crag and the mountain rescue men, with the stretcher, were winched down from the hovering craft to the screes to organize its installation. Strapped into our seats, with our crash helmets and radio equipment, we saw and heard everything and greatly admired the efficiency and professionalism of the crew, the mountain rescue men and the assisting climbers – about 25 in all. For me, a most exciting, although poignant, return to a familiar crag where I had first climbed more than 70 years ago.

CHAPTER NINE

Record Breaker

I N 1976 THERE WAS a grand retirement party for Harry Griffin thrown by the *Lancashire Evening Post* and he was presented, to his great delight, with the traditional commemorative front page made up by journalists to honour a particularly distinguished colleague. Its main headline read: 'Demob day for AHG – Lakeland's colonel of a million words.' But this was no real retirement and there were to be at least another half-million words. There may have been a fulsome tribute from the editor Barry Askew, who later went on briefly to take charge of the *News of the World*; and there was certainly an impressive guest list of Harry's contacts and friends for the dinner, including a former BBC governor, Lord Wilson of High Wray, and Detective Chief Superintendent Joe Mounsey, who arrested the Moors Murderers. But it was more significant that the commemorative page flagged up his continuing weekly Leaves from a Lakeland Notebook column, as well as two books, one just published and the other in preparation, compiled from his journalism for the *Post* and his *Guardian* Country Diary.

It was a case of onward and, needless to say, upward, as Harry hadn't long before celebrated his 60th birthday with a felltop walk of 45 miles instead of his more usual 20. Even what he called a bad year for outings, such as 1981 which was plagued with dismal weather and, for Harry, ill health, saw him on the fell summits 'only' 60 times. Back at home, he worked patiently and usually with enjoyment through another mountain, this one of correspondence from readers generated by his column. The *Guardian*'s circulation had risen from some 150,000 copies a day when he joined, to a peak of over half-a-million. One day would see an erudite inquiry from an Edinburgh professor about a Greek inscription on a mountain memorial. Another would ask for clues about places Harry had mentioned or guess at the identity of characters he had described but kept anonymous. He would usually give in to these often impassioned appeals. He never wanted to be a guidebook, directing people to the Lakes without any effort on their part. This was where he took issue with Wainwright who made it so easy that walkers armed with his books did not even need a compass (something Wainwright himself never knew how to use). But when readers took the trouble to write and give evidence that they had tried manfully to find one of his little nooks, his heart softened. Hundreds of them were quietly told by post that a marvellous hidden scramble on which he stumbled in the Eastern fells was the north-east ridge of Rainsbarrow Fell. This is the route described in Chapter 4 of this book, in the diary entitled 'A Hidden Gem'. I have kept Harry's identification of it until this chapter in his spirit of not making things too easy.

As milestone after milestone fell to Harry's Diary progress, several readers suggested that he deserved a place in the *Guinness Book of Records*. Unfortunately, even at the end of his 53-year run, this reckoned without the even greater marathon of Auntie Rhona of

the *Peterborough Standard*, a Miss Rhona Chesters whose Children's
Corner appeared weekly for more than 55 years. This was mildly
irritating to Harry, who like most climbers and walkers had something of the peak-bagger in his nature, but he consoled himself that
the *Peterborough Standard* was one thing and the *Guardian* another. He
had also written more books about the Lake District than anyone
else, and when his latest, *The Coniston Tigers*, was published in 1999 it
outsold every other title in the *Guardian*'s mail-order shop apart from
a new collection of poetry by the Nobel laureate Seamus Heaney.

Auntie Rhona was not striding up 3000ft mountains either, or
belaying a comrade on a vertical pitch of Dow Crag. These Harry
continued indomitably to do. In correspondence with the *Guardian*,
he emphasized how concerned he was to maintain his tradition of
writing 'about what happened the other day' rather than too many
nostalgic returns to the adventures of his youth. Eventually, he
admitted, he might have to settle for 'humbler pieces on crawling
about the lower fells', but not yet.

He was frequently in correspondence with the *Guardian* in these
later years, often in a state of fury at indignities inflicted on his
prose. To his lasting sadness, the Country Diary was finally moved
from its time-honoured place below the leaders. In the 1980s it
became a vagabond, moving about from section to section, finding
different editors and sometimes falling into what Harry considered
clumsy hands. His meticulous use of paper sized to exactly diary
length had transferred to his new word processor, on which he
carefully wrote exactly 27 lines. But in London, he told me in a
letter, this care encountered 'myriad balls-ups which I suppose is
normal these days'. One of his editors, Tim Radford, wrote
begging him to phone his copy to avoid the stresses of delayed post.
Another, Patrick Ensor, promised to stay late on Sunday nights to
see the diaries safely through sub-editing shifts which were sometimes manned by freelance casuals.

The protests were usually justified but sometimes they had the hallmark of increasing age. His readers, to whom he was devoted, got their share of flak, especially when they asked for free information – 'No one sends stamped, addressed envelopes,' he grumbled in 2000. He also gunned for politicians. His friendship with Lord Wilson of High Wray went back to his introduction to Kendal Rotary in 1949 by Wray, then a local businessman who gave a talk entitled 'Why I vote Labour'. But when Labour returned to power in 1997 after years in opposition, Harry wrote to a reader who was also a friend: 'Everybody thinks this New Labour government is wonderful. I wouldn't trust any of them, least of all this smarmy Blair; but the Conservatives, under this little lad, Hague, are a spent force, and we'll have to have to put up with New Labour for some years yet. Isn't politics a filthy business?'

Life was a see-saw. That same year saw Harry awarded the MBE for services to the Lake District and literature (the latter being the part of the accolade which made him really proud). At the same time, he was lamenting the loss of one of his great consolations, the piano. A bad fall on the Howgills broke two of his right fingers and he could no longer play.

Reminiscences began to play more of a part in his writing, both in the diaries as well as several 'Grand Old Man' pieces which were commissioned for him to look back over 30, 40 and then 50 years. His favourite quotation in these was A.P. Wadsworth's instruction to his new recruit to the eight-strong stable of Country Diarists: 'Write what you like but for heaven's sake keep off birds. We get all we want about them from the others.' As the years went by, Harry's eyebrows lifted and his eyes flashed as he listed the birds – pigeons, peregrine falcons, owls – which he had managed to fly through Wadsworth's, then Hetherington's, Preston's and Rusbridger's nets.

Mountain codgers
❧ MAY 1991 ☙

Four old but young-at-heart mountain men with ages totalling 300 years – the eldest is 84 – strolled lazily over the side of Green Quarter Fell to Skeggles Water and back down by a different way. One of us walked with the aid of two ski sticks, another used a stout ash for support, the third had appliances in his boots but the fourth, the youngest, seemed normal. It might have been an episode from *Last of the SummerWine* and, indeed, my woolly cap, picked up on the fells years ago, is rather like Compo's. Between us we probably have an unrivalled knowledge of the fells but we argued, in the friendliest way, about the way up and the best way down and failed to reach complete agreement about the horizon panorama from the highest point. We could all identify all the summits all round the compass; it was the minutiae of the distant scene – whether, say, it was a crag on Esk Pike that blocked the Great End cliffs – that caused the disagreement, so we agreed to differ. A superb corner below a little crag that sheltered us from a biting wind – there had been snow flurries earlier – provided an ideal luncheon spot, commanding a splendid view of the sunlit dale of the Kent and the familiar heights beyond. Here, over sandwiches and coffee, we discussed old climbs, long walks and ski trips of younger days. There was little sighing over lost youth but, rather, contentment that we could still get into the hills in our own fashion. Skeggles Water is, by no means, the most beautiful tarn in Lakeland but it is certainly one of the least frequented – an important consideration. We saw no sign of the whooper swans that stay there over winter but there were black-headed gulls and skylarks overhead. At least we were agreed on one point – that it had been a good thing that the plan to mine diatomite here many years ago was turned down.

Return to Scotland
∽ JULY 1993 ∼

Roadside banks of flaming gorse lighted much of our way up into the Highlands and, with the blue hills rising ahead, assured us we were really back in Scotland again – my annual retreat for nearly 60 years. One reason for this visit was to introduce a companion to Ben Nevis, the highest mountain in the British Isles but little more than a long and tiresome slog by the tourist route. We were an unlikely pair – an octogenarian geriatric and a great-grandmother with limited mountain experience – but we made it on a bad day of thick cloud and driving rain with about 5ft of visibility on the summit. In younger days I rarely used the tourist route which is now even more stony and unpleasant than I remembered so this will be my last ascent of the Ben. Other days were rather more scenically rewarding although less meritorious – an ascent of Aonach Mor, but half of it by gondola, and ascents of Cairn Gorm and Cairn Lochan, with considerable assistance from chairlifts. From these summits, all around 4000ft, views over much of Scotland were enjoyed but we had no time to collect Benn Macdui, the second highest mountain in Britain, having wasted most of the day waiting for the clouds to lift. Merely motoring holidaymakers probably found the weather, day after day, delightful but, with the highest tops covered in cloud for much of the time, we felt ourselves restricted and were even reduced to looking at ospreys from the Loch Garten hide or trying out the whisky at Tomintoul, the highest village in the Highlands. It was delightful crunching through summer snow again and identifying favourite hills of 50 years ago but next time we will avoid the popular places. We must have encountered, dimly seen in the mist, at least a hundred people on Ben Nevis, despite the poor conditions, and the chairlifts were busily rattling away all day in the Cairngorms. One elderly retired gentleman, met during our descent of the Ben, told me he believed, and hoped, he had been the oldest person on the summit that day. He had been deceived by the woolly 'Compo' tea-cosy covering my balding pate and I felt a little naughty telling him I had beaten him by 17 years. Aviemore, where I had spent my first honeymoon 56 years ago, has certainly changed in the intervening years but, even here, the recession seemed to be still biting.

A favourite corner
APRIL 1999

One of the most interesting, even exciting, corners of the fells is the square two or three miles of scarred and pock-marked country between Yewdale and the Brathay. Here is an area of low hills, scattered woodlands, old workings and surprises round every corner – no high mountains, great crags or lakes but, instead, some of the biggest holes in the Lake District, vaulted roofs like cathedrals and dark, forbidding pools. The whole area is rich in colour, history and wildlife – the early quarrymen hanging in chains as they hacked out the slate in dark holes, Lanty Slee distilling his potato whisky in remote caves, the smugglers with their ponies on the passes and, always, the watching excisemen. We were there again the other day, wandering over and around Holme Fell, one of the most complex little hills in the district, with widespread woodlands, scattered tarns, and, in its north-west corner, the tremendous man-made craters of Hodge Close. Climbers were practising abseiling on the soaring walls of the biggest hole, high above the black pool far below, as an owl quietly winged its way through the dark woods. Earlier, at Oxen Fell, we had watched a red squirrel scurrying along the branches of an old oak and, near one of the tarns that used to be a reservoir, spotted a fine heron taking off for the Uskdale Gap. The views, considering the fell is only a thousand feet high, were quite remarkable – the sunlit Troutbeck fells, Fairfield and Helvellyn, the Langdale Pikes quite close, the full length of Coniston Water and, seemingly almost overhanging us, the craggy east face of Wetherlam. And from every farm and cottage came the fragrant whiff of woodsmoke – a nostalgic scent that, for a lifetime, has always identified for me both this wooded corner and the quiet lanes of lovely Dunnerdale.

Still scrambling
FEBRUARY 1997

Doddery, old climbers who still itch to get their fingers on a bit of rock now and again might enjoy a favourite way of mine up Coniston Old Man that avoids the wearisome stones and screes of the usual routes. So, too, might modest scramblers or even adventurous pedestrians. From the start of the grievously-eroded quarries route you turn right into Boulder Valley and, after disporting yourself on the Pudding Stone or some of the other huge boulders that boast climbing routes, you scramble up to Low Water Beck, seen splashing down slabs to the west. This is a great place in winter where you may well have to queue up before tackling the frozen fall but when there's no snow or ice about you can scramble easily up to the right of the slabs, avoiding the two waterfall pitches. Having reached Low Water, dramatically sited in its splendid winter corrie – a pleasant luncheon stop – you take to the wonderful rough slabs on the far side of the tarn and mount, either with abandon or caution, to near the top of Brim Fell. This is a magnificent ladder to the heights, equipped, throughout its several hundred feet, with the sort of neat, little holds that persuade you that you can still climb a bit and, just when you need it, the occasional jug handle. As you climb you watch the ultramarine pools below your boots getting smaller and smaller and more and more like an ink blob and even feel sorry for the pilgrims toiling up the rough and dusty tourist route on the far side of the corrie. The slabs are splendidly airy, perhaps with ravens circling around, but reassuringly safer in good weather, for the non-expert. From the top there's a short walk to the Old Man and an easy descent, first along the south ridge and then, perhaps at the trot, down the zigzags past Bursting Stone quarry to the car. With luck you'll have had the whole route to yourself.

Content to watch
◁◁ APRIL 1997 ▷▷

For many years Borrowdale, for me, was a climbing valley – especially on days when the Scafell and Gable crags were out of condition or the daylight hours too short – and I have the happiest memories of wonderful days on Shepherds Crag, Black Crag, Raven Crag and other exciting places. But advancing years have put most of these old haunts out of bounds and, instead, I have been rediscovering the tourists' Borrowdale – the 'Beethoven of the Dales' as I described it in an early book – and looking at delightful corners often ignored when seeking problems of verticality. Especially rewarding has proved the thickly wooded country threaded by the most beautiful reaches of the delectable Derwent – the Jaws of Borrowdale, considered by the great Wainwright to be the loveliest square mile in Lakeland. Plumb in the middle of this magic mile is the abrupt, rocky pyramid of Castle Crag where Millican Dalton – the Professor of Adventure, as he called himself – lived for much of the year in a cave in the quarries. You could tell when he was in residence by the thick plume of smoke from his campfire rising through the trees. I knew dear old Millican and his cave quite well and would often bump into him collecting his groceries at the little shop in Rosthwaite and trundling them off on his bicycle. Also within the area, but the other side of the Derwent, is the beautiful, rocky height of King's How summit, high above the Bowder Stone, dedicated to the memory of Edward VII. Forty years ago I was writing about 'the exquisite walk up to King's How on a summer evening' but I don't think I had been up there since until the other day. The steep path through the trees has been roughly paved but it is still a lovely walk and the rocky top an airy eyrie. But I envied the two climbers slowly inching up Black Crag at the head of Troutdale, a once favourite haunt, vicariously savouring their every move.

Golden jubilee
ᕈ JANUARY 2001 ᕈ

Today's diary exactly completes 50 years of my contributions from the loveliest corner of England, the Lake District. The first one appeared in the *Manchester Guardian*, as it was then, in the first days of 1951, when George VI was on the throne and Clement Attlee the prime minister. It was two years before Tony Blair was born. There have been 1300 of my diaries altogether – most of them about hills, sunlit snows, clouds suddenly swept away from a ridge, and the dale, far below, leaping up at you, exciting climbing and skiing days, long days walking the tops, mountain views, golden eagles, red deer and many other important things. Hundreds of people have written to me about these simple pieces and their letters encouraged me to carry on.

All the articles – except for a handful from the Alps and the Rockies – were written from a succession of homes in and around Kendal that always looked out to the hills. Indeed, from the windows of one home, from which 30 years of diaries were written, I could at one time – before Whitehall messed about with the counties – see hills in four counties.

Father Time, though, is unforgiving. I kept up my rock-climbing until I was 78, and carried on skiing until I was 80, but today I just potter about the hills – mostly little ones – in geriatric fashion. I know where to go for quietude when the district is choc-a-bloc with traffic, but my greatest concern will always be that Lakeland is not further despoiled by the excesses of mass tourism and the greed of big business. May I wish you all a wonderful New Year in the hills.

90 years young
◐ JANUARY 2001 ◑

My unexpected achievement in reaching 90 years of age today is largely due, I'm convinced, to almost 80 years of active involvement with mountains. Thousands of days of fresh air, wind and rain, sunshine and snow, can't have done me much harm and, for a long lifetime, there's been the exhilaration of the heights – even if they're only little hills now. It started as a small boy in school uniform, walking from Foxfield railway station to the top of Stickle Pike and back, and clearly remembering the pungent, sweet scent of woodsmoke sniffed from some farm near Broughton Mills. And today, the scent of woodsmoke always takes me back to lovely Dunnerdale. Soon afterwards, as a family, we went up Black Combe. Again, we had no boots, map or compass, and my father, the leader, had never been up a hill in his life before but we just clambered up until there was nowhere higher to go. My main memory of that trip is of looking down from the summit on the fields and villages, the Furness peninsula spread out below us like a map. That was the start of my continued interest in maps, especially mountain maps. Hundreds of hills and mountains were enjoyed in the following years, and then, in the late 1920s, I started rock and snow climbing and, some years later, skiing. Before foot problems restricted activities, I completed 60 adventurous years of climbing and more than 40 years of skiing. But enough about me. I'm afraid we nonagenarians do go on a bit. But

I'm more fortunate than most, for I've managed to live within sight
of hills for most of my life and intend to crawl about on them for
as long as I can, God willing.

A deserted honeypot
MARCH 2001

Tarn Hows, the most popular tourist 'honey pot' in Lakeland, was
completely deserted the other day with mine the only car and not
a single walker. The weather was perfect – unbroken sunshine all
day, cloudless, blue skies and patches of snow on the fells – but
nobody around to enjoy it. The terrible scourge of foot and mouth
had cleared the countryside. There was no restriction on driving
down and past the tarn, although all car parks were closed, but you
were not allowed off the tarmac on to the paths. Tarn Hows is a
place I usually avoid, because of the crowds, but it is, although an
artificial creation, one of the most beautiful corners in Lakeland –
especially when you have it to yourself. From the top of the hill
leading down to the tarn, the craggy, east face of Wetherlam, almost
filling the western sky, seemed to soar like an Alpine peak above the
woodlands ringing the tarn, while a couple of swans decoratively
cruised the mirrored waters. Previous visits, begun nearly 80 years
ago, were mostly for the skating when the sheltered tarn,
surrounded by snowbound fells, seemed a winter paradise. We
lunched, the other day, in a lofty, country inn which looked across
at the sunlit Fairfield Horseshoe, and then, from Tarn Hows, drove
round Coniston Water, with its many memories dating back to
boyhood days. We passed, in turn, Arthur Ransome's 'Wildcat
Island', the place where Donald Campbell somersaulted to his
death and, on the other side of the lake, the site of our old,
wooden hut from where, before the war, we explored the climbs
on Dow Crag. Happier, less troubled days.

The hills re-open
৯৬ JUNE 2001 ৯৫১

Most of the high fells, out of bounds for 14 weeks, will be reopened this weekend and, at long last, much of our freedom of the hills will be restored. Where should we go for my first real walk, after months of promenade and tarmacadam bashing – the Scafells, Helvellyn or the Langdale fells? I think it will be the Coniston tops, a favourite corner since boyhood, with – if I feel up to it at 90 years of age – a walk along the airy top of Dow Crag where I began my rock climbing exactly 72 years ago. Starting from the fell gate above Coniston, it is a splendidly invigorating short round – up Walna Scar to the pass and then north along Brown Pike and Buck Pike to the rocky turrets of Dow Crag with its familiar gullies and walls plunging for nearly 1000ft to the black pool of Goats Water below the screes. Far down to the left are the wooded delights of the Duddon valley; due north the massive whale-backs of Skiddaw and Blencathra; and, below the sunset, the purple ramparts of the Scafells. There will be a thousand memories of great days as we tread the rocky ridge, climbers inching up the buttresses far below on routes that used to be more familiar to me than town streets. Most Dow days finished with the trot down the fellside to the Walna Scar track as the evening shadows lengthened and the ravens swooped over the crag. I can't think of a more stimulating return to the fells – an airy tramp along a rocky ridge I've known since boyhood, with peeps across to the roof of England. And I want to have another look at the stretcher-box memorial to my son – bright blue against the grey of the rock at the foot of the climbs.

Christmas mourning

❧ DECEMBER 2001 ❧

The last day of a terrible year in the fell country – the thousands of little tragedies in the hills, the strangely deserted sheep pastures, the smoke from the burning pyres desecrating the lovely landscape, the fells out of bounds for much of the year, tourism sorely threatened and, after September, nothing but talk of vengeance and war.

I remember long months when mountain folk, denied the heights, had to trudge instead along traffic-congested roads. Memories of Morecambe promenade and the struggle from Ambleside to Kirkstone and back come flooding in as well as a few pleasant trips along neglected country lanes – especially Paddy Lane, high above Kendal, with its glorious Lakeland views from the shoulder of Benson Knott. Then, in late October, a return trip to a favourite pre-war haunt, the beautiful Isle of Arran, spoiled by the often lovely autumn weather at its wettest worst.

Most clearly, I recall yesterday's Christmas tramp up and around the golf course behind my house. Here is one of the 'lungs of Kendal' where you can breathe mountain air after a short walk from the town streets, all a-glitter with the Christmas lights. There was a dusting of new snow on the Howgills and the High Street fells but hardly a speck on the Scafells and the Coniston hills, since the cold weather was coming in from the east. The ground was rock hard, the pools and puddles frozen over and the wind bitingly cold. There was nobody about and the low sun cast long shadows across the deserted greens. Just behind Gragareth the top of Ingleborough peeped up and smiled down. I was sure 2002 would be a better year.

Access for all

February 2002

A reader from Surrey, facing up to his wife's newly limited mobility, has asked if I can suggest Lakeland outings, away from main roads, where he can push her wheelchair. Both, I gather, are keen lovers of the fell country and, despite this sad restriction, are anxious to continue their enjoyment as long as possible. I think their reaction to misfortune highly commendable and, in wishing them well, I will be sending them a few ideas in addition to those in the excellent little booklet produced by the National Park Authority.

Much has been done in the Lake District by this authority, the National Trust, Forest Enterprise and others to help people with limited mobility to enjoy the area, but much more could be done were more finance available. The popular circuit of Tarn Hows is now suitable for wheelchair users provided two strong pushers are available, but the superb circuit of Buttermere, although practicable for some of the way, cannot yet be completed by the disabled. Similarly, the scenic traverse of Loughrigg Terrace with the completed round along the lakeshore is not yet feasible for wheelchairs. But there are short sections of lakeshore paths suitable for the disabled on both sides of Windermere, as well as on Derwentwater and Coniston Water, and the remote beauty-spot of Blea Tarn now has access for wheelchair users.

One small step

October 2003

There's the famous Hillary Step, just below the top of Everest, the so-called 'Bad Step' on Crinkle Crags scampered over, unnoticed, by everybody until Wainwright made a meal of it and named it, and now the Griffin Step on Scout Scar above Kendal.

This latest small step on to the base of the 'Mushroom' shelter was recently added, at my instigation, by two workmen finishing off the splendid restoration of the shelter, after it had been vandalised by mindless hooligans. I pointed out to the two workmen, busily cementing the base as they knelt in the limestone chippings, that when you're in your 90s the high step on to the base is rather an effort. Could they, please, add an extra step at the south corner? This they kindly agreed to do and when I next passed that way, there it was, in just the right place.

This must surely be one of the finest viewpoints in England, for you can see at least 120 hills and mountains in the Lake District, Yorkshire and Lancashire from it, as well as less interesting features such as Blackpool Tower, far away across Morecambe Bay.

The handsome domed shelter – always known locally as the Mushroom – was originally built in 1911 to mark the Coronation of King George V, and the restored memorial was unveiled to commemorate the golden jubilee of his grand-daughter, the Queen. The outline of the hills, now etched on stainless steel to try to deter modern vandals, is most accurately drawn and embraces the complete 360-degree view. Walk up my little geriatric step to the new seating some fine day and admire the most extensive view in the country – but be careful of the sheer drop over to the west.

Absent friends
MARCH 2004

Two of my oldest mountain friends passed away, within days of each other, recently. Kendal-born Alice ('Jammie') Cross, widow of my oldest friend, Sid Cross, distinguished rock climber and mountain rescue leader, had been, in her day, the best woman climber in the country. She was the first woman to lead Central Buttress on Scafell Crag, at one time the hardest route in England and still a formidable climb, and was the only woman climber, so far as I'm aware, to be specially commemorated at Rheged, the impressive mountain discovery centre near Penrith.

For many years Jammie and Sid were 'mine hosts' at the Dungeon Ghyll Old Hotel in Langdale, which they transformed into England's undisputed climbing centre – if not Britain's. After Sid had passed away – commemorated by a fine seat with an outstanding view at the back of their property on Loughrigg – Josie and I would often take Jammie, with her little dog, for a run in the car, a gentle walk on the lower fells around Langdale she knew so well, and a modest pub meal. An additional plaque for Jammie on 'Sid's Seat' would be especially appropriate. They were a lovely couple.

My second old mountain friend to pass away – peacefully in his sleep at the age of 95 – was Jim Porter – the last of the Coniston Tigers of Dow Crag, apart from myself and one other. There were nine of us originally and Jim was our best climber – the only one able to lead the desperate Black Wall. Regrettably, after a terrible 200ft fall down the front of Gimmer Crag, Jim, a quiet, gentle man, who loved crags, never climbed again.

Two-and-a-half legs and three sticks
APRIL 2004

With every possible car parking space taken in Kentmere – in mid-week in April – we had to abandon our plan to walk to the reservoir, so, instead, backtracked towards Staveley and went up to lonely Skeggles Water. Between us I reckon we had two-and-a-half legs; I am now rather crippled in one leg and my companion, Don, has only one leg and a tin one. Three sticks, between us, helped, and we managed fine despite the rocky track.

The day was quite superb – familiar, sunlit fells rearing up all round us, the valley, far below, threaded by the Kent, reaching north to the wall of crags where it has its source, and the blue sky full of birdlife. A buzzard, with its characteristic mewing cry, soared and circled above our heads and, every so often, there was the sound and sight of the curlew while Don identified many other birds through binoculars. We were fascinated, too, by the evidence, in three or four places, that, unbelievably, this quiet, remote upland could once have been an industrial area. Huge artificial mounds, like tumuli, were dotted about – signs of iron smelting or charcoal burning – although we found no clues in the spoil. But the map shows 'lead mines (disused)' not far away, and, down in the valley, diatomite is mined.

The tarn, a pleasant place for a quiet hour's fishing, lies on a broad saddle between Kentmere and Longsleddale, the valleys of, respectively, the Kent and the Sprint, both long and lively. Many trails, for ponies or people, criss-cross the moor, suggesting this could once have been a populated area, but we saw only one person all day. Whooper swans stay at the tarn for months but we saw none this lonely day.

Out for a drive
ౘ JUNE 2004 ౙ

Having had to give up my car recently because of geriatric injuries – after 73 years of driving – it was delightful to be taken by a friend for a drive over Kirkstone Pass. Studying, from the inn, the familiar rocky front of Red Screes – the nearest summit over 2500ft in Lakeland to a motor road and alcoholic refreshment – I recalled dozens of visits in all months of the year. But not nearly so many as those of Don Austin of Windermere. When I first met him, by chance, on the summit in the early 1980s, he told me this was his 199th visit. He seemed to be up there nearly every day. Our next casual meeting was a year or two later when I was descending a snow gully just to the left of Kilnshaw Chimney and almost stepped on his balaclava-ed head as he was climbing up. I can't remember whether or not I was wearing crampons at the time and can't guess how many hundred ascents Don must have completed by now.

I used to test myself, too, on Red Screes – initially, trying to reach the summit within an hour from my home, just outside Kendal, and, later, gradually reducing the time from the inn to the cairn. It proved comparatively simple to reach the summit within one hour from my home – the motoring used to take about 22 minutes – and I gradually whittled down the ascent of the rocky east face to half an hour and, eventually, to a minute or two less than this. A younger man – I was in my late 70s – or a fell runner would have been far quicker. Best to go up Red Screes in a snow-bound winter with the air so still you can hear voices down at the inn 1000ft below. But the colour of the shattered screes, giving the mountain its name, is most striking after rain.

CHAPTER TEN

Solace of the Hills

F ROM HIS EARLIEST days as a Country Diarist, Harry Griffin was an interested admirer of what he called 't'owd fowk' in his occasional rendering of Cumbrian dialect into prose. He noticed the dignity and grace of village elders enjoying a Westmorland dance and music festival in the summer of 1951. Repeatedly, he wrote elegant profiles of old dalesfolk – Whistling Jack Thistlethwaite, the 93-year-old photographer and climber Geoffrey Abraham who forms the subject of several diaries, the Skiddaw shepherd Pearson Dalton. They all seemed to be mellow and content at their great age.

In reality, as he admitted when his own turn came, it was not quite as picturebook as that to struggle with stiff joints, crippling asthma and the indignity of finding a simple stile awkward when a decade or so earlier he could swing up a cliff on half-inch deep handholds. Bit by bit, he had to abandon the skills which gave him his unique, high altitude place among British writers – 'unmatched above the 1500 contour', as his friend Norman Nicholson put it in an appreciative letter about one of the diaries. He had a nasty warning of things to come in an ascent of Broad Stand, the 'bad step' between England's highest mountain Scafell Pike and the neighbouring summit, Scafell. Halfway up the difficult patch, famously described by the poet Samuel Taylor Coleridge who bravely went this way in his solo tour of the tops in 1802, Harry's legs seized up. He lay there, flat against the rockface, looking like a frog with his knees locked in the breaststroke position. Remembering what he had been taught about cramp in the old Wastwater Hotel days, he searched his rucksack for anything salty and finally discovered a lump of mouldy cheese. He forced it down and the salt did its work, unlocking his legs so that he could finish the brief but taxing pitch. He gave up rock climbing, finally, at the age of 78 with a farewell ascent of a v. diff route on Grey Crag above Buttermere. He was still to scramble about and appear in photographs on what many armchair explorers would imagine to be a rock climb almost until the end of his days. There's one of him on what looks a precipice of slabs on Brim Fell above Low Water. But the real Coniston Tiger stuff was finished.

Skiing was next to go, with his last run at the age of 80, because his feet gave him too much pain to make this most favourite of all his outdoor activities endurable. When my photographer colleague Denis Thorpe and I went to interview him that year, we saw the awful agonies he went through in getting on, jamming on, his boots forcibly and with cries of pain. Once they were on, he was able to plod through the snow with us up the Kirkstone Pass, talking volubly as ever as we marched along. But it was heart-wrenching to be there as he got himself shod; and when he tried to ski the pain came back.

Gradually his horizons shortened. He read mountaineering books and the tales of Kai Lung, an adventure series set in China which Sandra tracked down in her various working places across the world. He might call in at Griffin's Bar, named in his honour at the Beech Hotel in Windermere. Or he would walk down into Kendal to a favourite rendezvous such as Smelly Nellie's for fish and chips, especially with his last devoted companion, Josie Clegg. When she died after nine loving years together, he was wrenched into despair once more. But he never gave up; and as he told the *Guardian*'s editor Alan Rusbridger, who succeeded Peter Preston in 1995, the discipline of the Country Diary helped to keep him going. He famously kept threatening to resign; as Northern Editor in Manchester and the nearest *Guardian* journalist to him physically, I fielded plenty of calls from him saying 'That's it,' usually after blunders such as Grasmere appearing as 'grassfire' or the reprinting of one diary a week later (not that readers minded the second chance to read his words). People will miss you terribly, I said – as did Alan in exchanges of letters, including one when Harry was in hospital for a spell, but still writing. So on he went. Talking in the year 2000 about his marathon stint with affection and endearing pride, he harked back to 1951 and sending his first contribution off to Cross Street. He added matter-of-factly: 'I was told to do it every other Monday after that and that's what I've done.'

He loved the routine; he was grateful that the commitment forced him out on the fells, or just out of doors, every fortnight; and in these last years, he became increasingly aware of the comfort he drew from the hills, the consolation for the loss of Mollie, Violet, Robin and finally Josie, who died of cancer at their flat in June 2003, the day before she was due to go into a Lancaster hospice. He retained his genial nature, enjoying the company of chance acquaintances on the fells such as a man wearing a 'radio hat' with dangling earplugs who initially flummoxed him with the greeting: 'We've avoided the follow-on' (he was listening to the Test Match). But seeing and remembering the wide sweeps of empty, lonely country had a special appeal. Then his own turn came, from cancer but quickly and peacefully in hospital with his last Country Diary safely in the post. His friend Canon Hodgkinson visited him on the evening of 8 July, and told us at the memorial service three weeks later: 'He greeted me warmly and was then very still whilst I blessed him. I whispered, "There are still many heights to conquer, Harry."'

You can imagine what that service was like, in one of the most beautiful parish churches in England, wide, low-slung ranges of mediaeval stone in green lawns on the banks of the Kent. Harry had written at the end of his mountaineering autobiography *The Coniston Tigers*: 'At least I can still lift up my eyes to the hills – every day,' and of course we sang those famous lines from Psalm 21. We also had Jerusalem, Wordsworth and the Ode to Joy which Harry used to play as a duet on the piano with Sandra. Then there was the Irish blessing hoping that the road would rise to meet you and – this being the Lake District – the rains fall softly upon your fields. Finally Canon Hodgkinson invoked that word 'transmogrified' – changed in an unexpected and magical way – with which Harry had rapturously greeted him when he learned to live again after Mollie's death. He told us: 'I like to think that he became young again and that when he saw the sheer beauty and infinite challenge of the heavenly mountains, that he was transmogrified.' To echo Harry's conclusion to his Country Diary on a day of sunshine and storm in June 1960, it was a good end to a good life.

Nobody goes there
⟡ SEPTEMBER 1964 ⟡

There was one day recently when the Lake District hills looked as sharp against the blue sky as if they had been cut out with scissors, when the smoke rose straight from the chimney pots in the valley and you could almost hear the insects talking. I was alone on the Dodds, those little-visited hills to the north of the Helvellyn range, and not only saw nobody all day but hardly heard a sound either. Three miles away, coach loads of tourists were noisily exploring Aira Force – I saw some of them on my way down – and I've no doubt there were processions going over Helvellyn, but nobody else had thought it worthwhile going up into these fells which look more blank on the map than any other part of the National Park except perhaps the bleak country at the back of Skiddaw. True, there's nothing very exciting about the Dodds, for there are no crags except some down by the road, no tarns to speak of – just a couple of pools – almost no sculpturing of the mountain sides, little bracken and heather, just miles of grass. But in place of the normal attractions there are the loneliness, the quietude, the splendid turf which makes such easy going, and the feeling that you can look out, around the whole compass, at the bigger mountains, as if from some upland promenade. Perhaps people knew these hills better 100 years ago, for last century coaches travelled an old road that contours round and the passengers would at last peer up the hillsides and maybe knew who was the Mr Watson of Watson's Dodd. And a thousand years earlier men were digging into one corner for lead. But today nobody goes there.

The solitary shepherd
∾ NOVEMBER 1969 ∾

For nearly half-a-century Pearson Dalton, a Lakeland shepherd, has lived alone with his dogs, goats and cat in what surely must be the loneliest house in England – 1600ft up in the untracked fell country at the 'back' of Skiddaw. In 1922 he went to Skiddaw House, a former shooting box nearly four mountain miles away from the nearest habitation, on a month's trial to look after the sheep and has stayed there ever since, through all the long winters of most memories – until the other day. But now Pearson, 75 years of age but still erect, strong and fit, has been compulsorily retired; his employer feels that should anything happen to the old man of the mountains he could be without help for days. And so, the other day, he collected his battered old radio set, his oil lamp, his sticks of furniture and his bedding and loaded them on to a farmer's jeep that had bumped up the track to the lonely house. Into the jeep went his cat, now 13 years old – his nannie goat, rumoured to be 22, had been moved a few days earlier – and Pearson, after a last bit of 'tidying up', looked at his home for the last time, and walked off over the hills into retirement with his five dogs at heel. He took the same route, six or seven miles northwards round the slopes of Great Calva to his sister's house near John Peel's Caldbeck, that he has been taking every Saturday for 47 years. This has been his link with civilization – his weekends among people as a change from his weekdays with rather more than a thousand sheep – and every Monday he has tramped back over the hills to Skiddaw House and five days of solitude – a well-contented man.

The hills is lonely

It was my first walk alone for a long, long time. The psalmist found help by lifting up his eyes to the hills but it didn't seem to work this lovely spring morning. I couldn't blame the view; the panorama from Lord's Seat on Whitbarrow, stretching from Black Combe to Ingleborough, cannot be excelled on a good day but, as somebody once wrote, 'the hills is lonely'. Gable peeped up to the right of Wetherlam, there were patches of snow on the distant top of Helvellyn, two buzzards soared lazily above Chapel Head Scar and the first primroses were out in the tangled woods below, but nothing cheered, not even the sunlight dancing on the estuary and the bird song in the trees. Near Raven's Lodge the vertical white cliffs and the terraced screes below could almost have been a corner of the Dolomites or even the steeps of Liathach. From the road these limestone escarpments look like white daubs painted across a green and brown fellside. But stand at their foot and they bulk and tower above you with frightening steepness. Thirty-six years ago they gave me a silver medal for getting two ewes off one of these crags but I couldn't find the place and it didn't matter. I've seen slim roe deer trotting daintily through these woods, silently slipping though the trees like shadows, but none today. No climbers either to watch on the beetling scar closed for the nesting season, a notice implied, so I was left with the fantastic view from the Hervey memorial cairn, surely the most embracing in England from a mere 700ft height. Easily I identified more than 30 summits, blue-remembered hills stretched all around the horizon, with even the Dow Crag gullies, 24 miles away, etched sharp against the morning sunlight.

Land without tracks

❧ JULY 1992 ❧

We saw nobody in the fells all day although it was a sunny Sunday, with cloudless blue skies and a pleasantly refreshing breeze. But then we were doing the round of the Bannisdale fells where, in many visits, I have never seen anybody and would have been surprised if I had. These undulating fells, immediately west of the Shap Fells road, form part of the loneliest corner of the national park. There are no tracks, apart from some at the northern end scratched out by motorcyclists – probably lads from the farms in the dale – no cairns and no sign of Man except for his ubiquitous dry-stone walls. The horseshoe round of up to 12 miles takes in half a dozen modest summits. The highest, about 1800ft, commands splendid views of most of the Lakeland fells, the Yorkshire hills and Morecambe Bay, and nicely fills in five or six hours of easy going – if you can cope with awkward tussocks of grass and heather. Ideally, Grey Crag, the most easterly two-thousander in Lakeland, should be included, adding a couple of miles to the round, but this time, feeling lazy, I resisted the temptation. Usually, it can be quite a boggy round but, the other day, the drought had made the going firm and dry. Often, too, you see fell ponies in these parts but not this time. Instead we watched one red deer, trotting nimbly through the heather just ahead of us, and a soaring buzzard, heard the skylarks and found a dead badger, badly mauled. I think it is the spaciousness and the wide horizons and the feeling you are on your own, miles from anywhere, that is so attractive but not, of course, to everyone. The views, too, are slightly different – the Scafells peeping up behind Bowfell and the Crinkles, Great Gable looking like a Christmas pudding and the unmistakable flat top of Ingleborough just showing over Middleton Fell. It is also interesting on horseshoe rounds like this to see where you've got to go or, looking across, where you've been. But, mostly, it's having mile after mile of unmatched scenery and vast skyscapes, without one harsh note or sound at all, except the birds, all to yourself.

Mrs Tiggywinkle's hill
MAY 1993

Old men with walking sticks, young children in gym shoes and even babies cocooned in fathers' rucksacks were on top of Catbells the other day and, in their dozens, wandering along the lazy ridge to High Spy. It was a perfect day for idling on the tops – warm and sunny, barely a breath of wind and matchless views to far horizons. The last drifts of snow were still clinging to the top of the north face of Helvellyn and later, from High Spy, we saw the last white handkerchiefs of winter on Great Gable. Catbells has always seemed, to me, a family hill for enthusiasts of all ages but mostly for children; it was, I recall, my daughter's first 'mountain', ticked off at the age of two-and-a-half. A pretty name for a child's mountain – the hill where Beatrix Potter's Mrs Tiggywinkle had some of her adventures, finally disappearing through a door somewhere Newlands way. And from the top, this bright afternoon, Keswick looked a fairy town in a magic landscape and Derwentwater, spread out below us like a pond, ringed with wooded fells and dotted with enchanted islands with white yachts becalmed as if floating butterflies, an exciting place for youthful adventure. We had to dawdle; there was so much to see and admire – the lovely, unspoiled Vale of Newlands and every step of the routes up Robinson and Hindscarth, the crumpled ram's horn shape of the summit of Causey Pike and its exciting ridge, the crowded woodlands and crags of Borrowdale with 60 years of adventurous memories and, straight ahead, a glimpse of the highest land in

England. Two jet aircraft streaked, in a sudden crash of sound, through the Jaws of Borrowdale below on our left and a pair of ravens, as always up here, performed aerobatics for us high above the perch of High Spy. We came down by Hause Gate, past the memorial seat for Hugh Walpole who lived in the lovely house, today carpeted with daffodils, on the lower slope of the fell looking out across the lake. Each morning, after breakfast, he would cross the lawn to his big library over the garage and write quickly, often describing scenes he could see from his windows, so that many of his heroes strode these grassy slopes or ran up through the bracken and the heather to watch the sun setting behind Grasmoor.

The empty heart of Lakeland
ꙮ August 1994 ꙮ

You can see Ullscarf from the limestone heights above my home – a long, whale-backed ridge over 20 miles away, well to the right of Langdale Pikes and High Raise. Although a superb viewpoint, it is an undistinguished fell but happens to have the distinction of being the most central of our two-thousand-footers – the very heart of mountain Lakeland. We went up from the shore of Thirlmere on a bright, warm day tempered by a fresh breeze – a trackless route working westwards through the bracken and round little crags towards the distant skyline, pausing now and again to look back at the vast bulk of Helvellyn crowding the eastern horizon. It is only from these fells west of the toe of Thirlmere that you can see the wide front of Helvellyn. There were two people sitting by the summit cairn on Ullscarf, a man and a boy, the only people we saw all day. It was their first visit to this fell and the first big hill for nine-year-old Andrew at the very start of his praiseworthy bid to collect all the two-thousanders. We wished him many long days in the hills.

Father and son went down the line of the broken fence to a rendezvous at Watendlath while we went in the opposite direction to Greenup Edge and back down the long length of Wythburn to the car. The view from Ullscarf on this bright day, when the clarity almost reached February perfection, was quite outstanding. Through a gap between Barf and Ullock Pike we could see into Scotland – Criffel and the Galloway hills – and, turning round, there was Ingleborough peeping over a shoulder of Gragareth. Wythburn was deserted and desolate as usual but since the inauguration of the Lakeland three-thousanders walk, with hundreds of people traversing this once-quiet dale every summer, a track of sorts now winds through the bogs and their passage is much easier. Lemon-coloured water lilies grace the tiny tarns in the bogs, and there is a lovely dale, threaded by splendid waterfalls and quiet pools, shaded by rowans with dragon-flies skimming the surface and, further down, sloping meadows dotted with clumps of nodding harebells.

The secret zigzags
❧ APRIL 1995 ❧

We reached our first summit, the Old Man, by the pleasant Bursting Stone ('Brussen Staen' to the locals) quarry route that cleverly zig-zags up the east face from Boo Tarn, ending, the other day, with a steep 500ft slope of beautifully-compacted snow that needed just one good kick for each step. In youthful days this was one of our 'secret' ways but 35 years ago Alfred Wainwright publicized it in one of his guides, waxing almost lyrical over the fascinating and unexpected zig-zags along terraces 'scented with thyme and tiny alpines'. He added: 'The man who worked out this delightful, well-graded and ingenious route . . . deserved a medal.' In fact, the architect of this useful track was my old school pal and fellow member of the Coniston Tigers climbing club, Jack Diamond, village schoolmaster in Coniston and an inveterate builder of huts and bothies in the fells – although he lived in their shadow. I remember him working on the route and enthusing about it; he preferred quiet ways and didn't care for the ugly, stony staircase through the big quarries where the crowds went. Sadly, Jack died many years age but his widow, Peggy, who helped him with the back-breaking job of building the dozens of cairns, is still alive. As we followed his route along the snow-covered terraces, the cairns in exactly the right places, I remembered my old friend and quietly thanked him for his enterprise, energy and public spirit. Boo Tarn was a tarn in those days – today it's just a muddy pool choked with reeds – and Bursting Stone was just a tiny derelict quarry. It was re-opened in about 1960 and vastly enlarged with a private road up the fellside. Another of Jack's cairned routes was a useful trod from Goats Hause to Levers Hause, cutting out the usually-crowded Old Man to Brim Fell highway; you never met anyone on this airy track above the crags. My own contribution to all this route-finding was a slightly adventurous traverse from Raven Tor to Low Water – originally worked out by sheep and still, I hope, uncairned. Unlike Jack I'm not a cairn-builder; there are far too many of these people about – builders of quite unnecessary cairns, not useful ones like those on the Bursting Stone route. But, on this bracing day of sunlit snows, I so far forgot myself that I added a couple of stones to one of Jack's piles of 50-odd years age – this time out of admiration and affection.

A special resting-place
NOVEMBER 1996

A mountain friend has directed his ashes should be scattered on Pen, his favourite Lakeland summit. It is also, certainly, one of mine – a remote height, possibly the least-visited summit in the district although only a rough half-mile away from the usually-crowded top of Scafell Pike. There's a Heaton Cooper painting of Pen hanging on a wall in my drawing room – the upper Esk rushing through boulders in the foreground, the sun illuminating the steep front of Esk Buttress and the knobbly top of Pen, just above, with the dark summits of the Pike and Ill Crag just shrouded in mist. I've been up there several times – first, 50 years ago, after a day's climbing on Esk Buttress – but have never seen anyone else in the area. There are no tracks to point the way and although the 2500ft-high summit is graced by a neat cairn, there are no beer-can rings, orange peel or sandwich wrappings to indicate the previous presence of civilized man. On all sides, little to see except crag and scree – not even grass. One visit, ticking off the 'two-thousanders' on a nasty day of wind and rain, involved a 700ft descent of steep scree from the Broad Crag col and a scramble to the top, with the reward of a brief lifting of the cloud on the summit. Far below, suddenly revealed, lay the tumbled wilderness of upper Eskdale and straight across the ravine of Little Narrowcove, the black cliffs of Ill Crag looking quite impregnable but, as we discovered on a later occasion, no more than a sporting scramble. A better way from Scafell Pike may be to descend steeply south-east from the summit but the best approaches are from upper Eskdale striking north from the river just to the left of the fine cliff of Esk Buttress, marked Dow Crag on the map. Higher up Little Narrowcove is another remote two-thousander, Rough Crag, probably only visited by devoted tickers of lists and not as dramatic a summit as Pen. My friend had well chosen the last resting place for his bones.

Christmas in Kendal

DECEMBER 1997

Hopefully not permanently, the hills are, regrettably, unavailable but at least I can look out of my windows. When I open my eyes in the morning, I see from my pillow, without raising my head, the recently-renovated ruin of Kendal Castle, atop a pleasant green hill – the birthplace of Katherine Parr, last (and surviving) wife of Henry VIII. Just to the left, beyond the town hall clock, bulks the sprawling 1000ft height of Benson Knott, a fine viewpoint with rather limited access. But the view in this direction, to the east, is mostly of rooftops – surprisingly attractive rooftops, too, especially when there's snow about, as there was last week, with all the Christmas lights and decorations bringing a touch of winter magic to the old town. Indeed, on some days, I feel I could almost be looking down on Kitzbühel or Klosters – an impression fortified by the sight of skiers on the town's artificial ski-slope, just beyond the roofs. Through binoculars I can almost identify the skiers or, at least, easily separate those who can ski from the beginners. From another window, looking north, I can see the fells – the long line of the Whinfell ridge from Ashstead Fell to Grayrigg Common, a favourite round when combined with the tramp through Westmorland's Borrowdale, and the hills around Bannisdale, mounting gently towards Grey Crag. As I look out now, this cold, frosty morning, the sun is shining on the lovely, little pointed peak of Whiteside Pike, not far to the left of the Shap Fells road. The view is nothing like so widespread and dramatic as that from the fellside home I left eight years ago, where I could see the big hills in four counties stretched out along the horizon, but at least I can see the cloud shadows racing across familiar fells and sense the mountain air. Things could be much worse.

Are the hills out of reach?

⤫ JULY 2003 ⤫

The realization that I have probably climbed my last hill only began to sink in a few days ago. Since the passing of my lovely Josie a few weeks ago, much physical deterioration has set in and I now have to accept the fact that the hills are really beyond me. But I can see some of them from my windows, and perhaps in the future I may be able to get a little closer, so all is not yet lost.

It is just 80 years since I climbed my first real hill, Stickle Pike in Dunnerdale, in a party of short-trousered second formers, and since then there have been many hundreds of mountain, rock and ice climbs, skiing days and thousands of dawns, sunsets and wonderment at the beauty of mountain country in many parts of the world. My last proper outing with Josie was towards the end of last October, when we did the three miles round Levens Park, seeing deer, goats, squirrels, swans, kingfishers and the glory of the changing colours of the trees. Our last hill walks, a little earlier, had been Loughrigg and Arant Haw in the Howgills and, at the end of the foot-and-mouth restrictions, we managed to get up Ingleborough, Josie's favourite mountain, once more.

If the *Guardian* is prepared to put up with these effusions – I've done almost 53 years of them – I'll try to carry on with my Country Diary even though I won't be describing adventures of the last week.

May I thank all the hundreds of readers who have written to me over the years – especially those who have tried to comfort me over Josie. I don't think I'll be able to reply but please keep on sending them. So many of you have asked me to carry on that I mustn't give up yet.

Yorkshire with Josie
 JULY 2003

Although my beloved Josie had climbed every mountain and fell in Lakeland, except two, as well as scores of others in northern England and Scotland, her favourite hill was not in the Lakes. It was Ingleborough, the bold, flat-topped monarch of the Yorkshire Dales, which you can just see, peeping over the shoulder of Gragareth, from the fell behind my house. She had first climbed it, with me, from Ingleton by way of the isolated farm of Crina Bottom on a bracing day with hard frost in January 1992.

As we were stepping down the upper slopes of millstone grit from the summit we met a man with a curious load on his back on his way to the top. Perhaps 20 minutes later, on the lower slopes of the hill, we heard a noise and the same man dropped, literally, at our feet in a hang glider, having jumped from the summit. We walked down together and were fascinated to hear about, and tempted by, the delights of this thrilling sport.

In the coming years Josie and I went up and down Ingleborough by six different routes, the next one being from Clapham and past the immense gulf of Gaping Gill. Just before reaching this enormous cavern I showed her the entrance to Bar Pot, one of the routes to the great chamber of Gaping Gill where, many years ago, as a novice potholer, I had taken part in the second descent of the route. I think Josie's favourite route to her favourite mountain was from Ribblehead and over Park Fell. Her last visit to Ingleborough was in October 2001, when it had just been reopened after the foot-and-mouth restrictions, and we were among the first to tread the new wealth of grass and flowers.

Farewell to Josie
NOVEMBER 2003

We made our last farewells to Josie on a bright, early-autumn day
that was so clear the hills on the horizon looked within throwing
distance. She had always wanted her ashes to be scattered on Lanty
Tarn, her favourite pool high above Ullswater, so four of us walked
up the steep, rocky way from Glenridding – her eldest daughter,
my daughter-in-law, my 'minder' to help me with any difficulties,
and myself, hobbling with a stick.

Since I had first introduced Josie to Lanty Tarn and explained its
original use to supply ice for the big house in the dale, and how it
came by its name, she had always been fascinated by the pool. She
even named a flat she once owned in Kendal, 'Lanty's', having the
name-plate carved in oak by a friend. We often visited the place,
perhaps on our way to Helvellyn, or, more often, on the morning
walk from Glenridding, over the little col and down past
Grassthwaitehow and the kennels of the Ullswater foxhounds into
Grisedale, and the pleasant walk back along wooded paths. There
are many photographs of Josie standing elegantly by the tarn with
the trees perfectly reflected in the water but, on this last visit, the
picture was not so impressive, the dry summer having shrunk the
size of the pool.

We had our quiet, little ceremony, thinking about our wonderful
Josie, who always thought about other people, never herself, and will
never be forgotten. Then we walked up the adjoining, little hill of
Keldas with its superb view of the length of Ullswater framed
between two old Scots pines. At the end, we walked down the hillside, not saying very much but thinking a lot. Lovely, little Lanty
Tarn will always mean everything to me.

Another milestone

❧ DECEMBER 2003 ☙

This piece exactly completes 53 years of these fortnightly effusions. It was towards the end of 1950 that the editor of the then Manchester *Guardian*, A.P. Wadsworth, told me: 'Write about anything you like but, for God's sake, keep off birds. We get enough about these from the others' – meaning the other Country Diary writers, now, I fear, all translated into the upper air.

For many, myself included, this has been a very sad year, and the ending of it seems especially difficult to endure with everybody so happy about Christmas. But one day at this tail-end of a year that has provided such a wealth of outdoor beauty eased the sadness for a while. From a hill high above Kendal I looked down on the old, grey town spread out like a map below me. The town, I knew, would be choked with traffic – it always is – and loud with noise but, from this height, not a sound could be heard, nothing moved, or so it seemed, and the place looked like a fairy town, bedecked with lights, where everyone must be happy and healthy. It had frozen heavily during the night and my hill, and all the rooftops far below, were white with hoarfrost.

Then – it was on the hour – I could hear, very, very faintly, the chimes of the carillon high up in the town hall clock and it sounded as if the fairies were ringing the bells. Nothing could be bad, or ugly or sad, with that fairy music winging its way across the fells, so, feeling a little better, I looked north-west across the new whiteness at Scafell Pike, rearing up behind the Crinkles, and the rounded dome, like an atomic cloud-burst, of Great Gable – both of them ablaze with the setting sun. Now, life seemed worthwhile.

Harry's final diary

❧ MONDAY, 12 JULY 2004 ❧

People were always asking me to name my favourite mountain in the Lake District – an impossible task. All I could say was that it was the mountain on which I happened to be at the time. Great Gable, Scafell Pike, Coniston Old Man and many others were considered but all had to be rejected. But now, well into my 90s, I feel forced to name a favourite and have decided to plump for Black Combe which, to some people, is not a mountain at all since it does not attain the magic 2000ft. But to my younger brother and me it was always a mountain, rising like a great whale and filling the sky to the west of our home at Barrow-in-Furness. We thought the Black Combe – best seen in winter when the snow outlined its shape – was an extinct volcano. One day in about 1924 we were staying with our parents at the inn at Green Road, just south of Black Combe, and decided to go up the mountain. But my father would not allow us to go alone, saying we were too young, so to solve the problem he would accompany us.

We were an unlikely trio for mountaineering – we had no boots, no maps and no mountain gear at all – and our father had never been on any mountain in his life. So we just walked a couple of miles along the main road – and then straight up the fell where we never found a single track. Most surprisingly, we reached the summit, and looked north-east at the Lakeland fells, then at the miles of shore and sand – no Sellafield then, of course – and finally our home town, Barrow, with the bridge to Walney Island and all the cranes spread out like a map far below us. We neither knew nor cared that Wordsworth had described the view as the most expansive in the country.

(Denis Thorpe, courtesy of Guardian Newspapers)

POSTSCRIPT

TOWARDS THE END of Harry's marathon stint, his thoughts turned to the question of a successor. The job was not in his gift but the *Guardian* was much too polite to raise the issue, and he was conscious of George Muller's probable role in his own appointment so many years before. He also had just the person in mind, a Yorkshireman living in Kendal called Tony Greenbank, who took up rock-climbing after overhearing Harry talking about it in the town library where he was working at the time. Now 70 and a freelance journalist, his other distinctions include helping Harry to master his first computer at the age of 87. Here is his first *Guardian* Diary, a warm tribute to his mentor and friend.

Follow in his footsteps
26 JULY 2004

I left the car above Coniston with a heavy heart. The track ahead was rutted, rock-strewn, crag-bound. It twisted across a barren fellside in the gathering dusk. Suddenly, as I topped a rise, Valhalla sprang into view: Dow Crag itself. The five buttresses of the giant precipice rose, their liquorice-black tops serrated against the sky; below the cragface, silvery scree spilled down into Goats Water, the lonely tarn below.

Seated on a boulder by the outlet, I remembered Harry Griffin as we had once sat here eating our sandwiches before reaching the crag overhead and roping up. He had pointed out the climbs of his youth: Arete, Chimney and Crack on A Buttress, and there, across Great Gully, on B Buttress, was the quartz flash on Giant's Crawl which looks like eternal snow, and Woodhouse's Climb nearby, his maiden route. And Tiger Traverse, a 'delicate' slab up which he was to tiptoe in pumps as one of the first climbers in 1931; still rated today as a life-threatening piece of rock. The Coniston Tigers were his peers, a 'gang of crag rats', who had escapades galore.

He had recently told me that he had considered including me in his will, but then changed his mind. He said it would be better, instead, if I could follow his path and write these diary pieces when he retired. In daylight he had shown me ways to bypass the stony path to Dow, via this sheepfold and that quartz cairn, cruising on emerald turf. There was no chance of finding these gems now as I retreated downhill guided only by the grooves cut by innumerable boot soles in the track, until, with a start, I bumped into the car.